ELEMENTS OF Literature

FIRST COURSE

LANGUAGE AND WRITING SKILLS WORKSHEETS

ANSWER KEY

HOLT, RINEHART AND WINSTON

Harcourt Brace & Company

Austin • New York • Orlando • Atlanta • San Francisco • Boston • Dallas • Toronto • London

1997 Reprint by Holt, Rinehart and Winston, Inc.
Copyright © 1995 by Holt, Rinehart and Winston, Inc.

Portions of this work were published in previous editions.

Printed in the United States of America

ISBN 0-03-095735-4

1 2 3 4 5 6 082 99 98 97 96

Table of Contents

Writer's Quick Reference

◆ WORKSHEET 1: COMMON USAGE PROBLEMS A

Exercise A
1. altars; everywhere
2. altogether
3. advice
4. advise
5. alter

Exercise B: Revising
1. Oh, no! I can't find my wallet anywhere!
2. Do you know where the conference room is?
3. I've been waiting for an 8:00 bus for an hour.
4. No, I'm not going to lend you a dollar.
5. C

◆ WORKSHEET 2: COMMON USAGE PROBLEMS B

Exercise: Proofreading
(The first item in each pair is the incorrect usage in the sentence. The second item is the corrected usage.)
1. between—among
2. capitol—capital
3. C
4. brake—break
5. bad—badly
6. bust—break
7. among—between
8. capital—capitol
9. C
10. C

◆ WORKSHEET 3: COMMON USAGE PROBLEMS C

Exercise A
1. cloths
2. council
3. counsel; course
4. course

Exercise B: Revising
1. Why doesn't she at least fold her own clothes?
2. You could have called if you were going to be late.
3. The new model has fewer moving parts and is more reliable.
4. A camel's large feet give it good footing in the shifting sands of the desert.

◆ WORKSHEET 4: COMMON USAGE PROBLEMS D

Exercise A: Proofreading
(The first item in each pair is the incorrect usage in the sentence. The second item is the corrected usage.)
1. C
2. hear—here
3. good—well; had ought—ought
4. good—well

Exercise B: Revising
1. Class had hardly started when the fire alarm went off.
2. It's ten o'clock; you ought not to be calling them this late.
3. Why do you understand usage so well?
4. Don't help him; he has to learn to think for himself one day.

◆ WORKSHEET 5: COMMON USAGE PROBLEMS E

Exercise: Proofreading
(The first item in each pair is the incorrect usage in the sentence. The second item is the corrected usage.)
1. kind of—rather *or* somewhat
2. learn—teach
3. like—as
4. passed—past
5. outside of—outside
6. lose—loose
7. lead—led
8. loose—lose
9. C
10. led—lead; inside of—inside

◆ WORKSHEET 6: COMMON USAGE PROBLEMS F

Exercise A
1. try to
2. plane
3. peace
4. peace; piece
5. Plain

Exercise B: Proofreading
(The first item in each pair is the incorrect usage in the sentence. The second item is the corrected usage.)
1. real—very *or* extremely
2. too—two; some—somewhat
3. try and—try to
4. threw—through
5. C

◆ WORKSHEET 7: COMMON USAGE PROBLEMS G

Exercise
1. week; who's
2. that
3. your
4. unless
5. that; whose
6. which
7. who
8. You're
9. that
10. whether

◆ WORKSHEET 8: THE DOUBLE NEGATIVE

Exercise: Revising

(Answers may vary.)

1. Nobody in our family had ever eaten any enchiladas before that night.

2. No, I haven't seen Pia anywhere at school.

3. "We haven't got anything to do," whined the bored seven-year-olds.

4. Neither of the children had spotted any rabbits that night.

5. It hardly ever snows here.

◆ WORKSHEET 9: REVIEW

Exercise A

1. advice
2. led
3. himself
4. Through
5. lose
6. very
7. who
8. passed
9. break; two
10. It's; could have

Exercise B: Revising

1. Bike riders ought to know some simple rules of safety.

2. The pilot must quickly decide whether to parachute to safety or try to land the crippled plane.

3. Your dog is too sleepy to learn any new tricks.

4. Spring break starts next week.

5. My mother and father both took part in Operation Desert Storm.

6. You should use soft cloths to clean silver.

7. C

8. One of the purposes of the Cabinet is to advise the president.

9. Why did you choose dinosaurs for your science project?

10. Yes, there are still openings in the karate course that I'm taking.

Exercise C: Revising

(Answers may vary.)

1. He doesn't know anything about it.

2. That couldn't have happened anywhere around here.

3. We didn't have any directions, so we got lost.

4. The meeting had hardly started when an angry man walked in.

5. Until then, none of us had ever been to a circus.

Chapter 1: Parts of Speech

◆ WORKSHEET 1: TYPES OF NOUNS A

Exercise A

1. sun, star
2. sister, student, chemistry, summer
3. Mr. Morales, koalas, trip, Australia
4. Suke, goalie, team
5. Janell, party, play
6. parents, Hawaii, convention
7. storm, game, World Series
8. actors, faith, director
9. Lucy, chimpanzee, words, sign language
10. Ryan, humor, essays

Exercise B

1. Rebecca Motte, patriot
2. Revolutionary War, soldiers, mansion, South Carolina
3. General Harry Lee, Motte, Americans, home, enemy
4. Motte, plan, country
5. arrows, bow, attack
6. enemy, flag, surrender, house
7. Motte, soldiers, sides, dinner

◆ WORKSHEET 2: TYPES OF NOUNS B

Exercise A: Revising

(Answers will vary.)

1. The *Mona Lisa* is in the Louvre.

2. Officer Martinez directed us to the Federal Building on Main Street.

3. Aunt Sally and Uncle Bill, who are from Butte, now live in Chicago.

4. Mr. Ellman asked Jerry to return *A Wizard of Atuan* to the Johnson Memorial Library.

Exercise B

(Sentences will vary.)

1. concrete—Soy sauce is good on all kinds of food.

2. abstract—The crowd's excitement mounted as the players were introduced.

◆ WORKSHEET 3: TYPES OF PRONOUNS A

Exercise A

1. I—Ms. Gaines; you—class
2. her—firefighter
3. themselves—children
4. they—Jenny, Rosa

Exercise B

1. We—P; ourselves—R
2. I—P; us—P
3. himself—I; me—P
4. itself—R

◆ WORKSHEET 4: TYPES OF PRONOUNS B

Exercise

1. who—REL
2. one—IND; that—REL
3. Everyone—IND; who—REL
4. Whom—INT
5. What—INT
6. all—IND; these—DEM
7. no one—IND
8. this—DEM
9. one—IND; who—REL
10. what—REL

◆ **WORKSHEET 5: ADJECTIVES A**

Exercise A

1. an—I; older
2. The—D; sudden
3. a—I; small, electric
4. a—I; medium, extra
5. The—D; mysterious

Exercise B

Adjective	*Word Modified*
1. horror	story
2. imaginative	plot
3. One	night
stormy	night
several	stories
4. scary	stories
5. terrible	night
6. all	night
strange	nightmare
7. young	doctor
8. ghastly	nightmare
9. eerie	novel
great	success
10. Several	movies

◆ **WORKSHEET 6: ADJECTIVES B**

Exercise A

1. Many—C
2. small—C
3. clever—C
4. South American—P
5. small—C
6. bony—C
7. delicate—C
8. narrow—C
9. tough—C
10. Asian—P

Exercise B

(Sentences will vary.)

1. Mexican food is sometimes hot and spicy.
2. The Memorial Day parade featured marching bands playing patriotic music.
3. Tomorrow, candidates from the Sixth Congressional District will debate the issues of concern to the voters.
4. The Hawaiian landscape is lush with tropical plants and trees.
5. Professor Park showed us photographs of the Korean countryside.

◆ **WORKSHEET 7: NOUN, PRONOUN, OR ADJECTIVE?**

Exercise A

1. A   3. A   5. A   7. P   9. P
2. P   4. N   6. A   8. A   10. N

Exercise B

1. some—P; this—A; good—A; Texas—A; barbecue sauce—N [or barbecue—A; sauce—N]; that—A; sandwich—N
2. Sam Houston—N; president—N; Texas—N; it—P; state—N
3. Allison—N; white—A; dress—N; dance—N
4. This—A; town—N; good—A; dress—A; shop—N [or dress shop—N]

5. Many—A; people—N; many—P; these—A; festivals—N

◆ **WORKSHEET 8: ACTION VERBS**

Exercise A

1. built
2. explained
3. enjoy
4. drops
5. skidded
6. made
7. Mix
8. delayed
9. gave
10. worshiped

Exercise B

Letters will vary but should include at least ten action verbs, three of which express actions that cannot be seen.

◆ **WORKSHEET 9: TRANSITIVE VERBS AND INTRANSITIVE VERBS**

Exercise A

1. I   3. T   5. T   7. T   9. I
2. I   4. I   6. T   8. T   10. T

Exercise B

(Sentences will vary.)

1. I flew a <u>kite</u>.
   The kite flew overhead.
2. She left the <u>club</u>.
   We left yesterday.

◆ **WORKSHEET 10: LINKING VERBS**

Exercise A

1. felt—L
2. resigned—A
3. seemed—L
4. fought—A
5. ended—A

Exercise B

Linking Verb	*Words Joined*
1. looked	animals . . . content
2. sounds	voice . . . human
3. grew	farmers . . . fearful
4. are	Some . . . old
5. is	mine . . . museum

◆ **WORKSHEET 11: THE VERB PHRASE**

Exercise A

1. <u>have been</u>
2. <u>have been destroyed</u>; <u>is being threatened</u>
3. <u>might . . . have been saved</u>
4. <u>will have disappeared</u>
5. <u>can . . . be saved</u>

Exercise B

1. would <u>buy</u>
2. would <u>hold</u>
3. were <u>described</u>
4. have <u>celebrated</u>
5. was <u>declared</u>

◆ **WORKSHEET 12: ADVERBS THAT MODIFY VERBS**

Exercise A

1. <u>once</u> <u>lived</u>
2. <u>hurried</u> <u>excitedly</u>
3. <u>totally</u> <u>ignored</u>
4. <u>Later</u> <u>were forced</u>
5. <u>were</u> <u>hardly given</u>

Exercise B

(Answers will vary.)

1. The victorious knight proudly rode his horse across the drawbridge.
2. People cheered wildly as he entered.

◆ WORKSHEET 13: ADVERBS THAT MODIFY ADJECTIVES AND ADVERBS

Exercise

1. probably—is
2. outdoors—goes; terribly—cold
3. completely—alone; alone—is traveling
4. Foolishly—confident; unusually—harsh; not—does understand
5. quite—instinctively; instinctively—knows
6. fearfully—slinks; along—slinks
7. Soon—are frosted
8. desperately—builds
9. Unfortunately—falls; suddenly—falls
10. now—know

◆ WORKSHEET 14: ADJECTIVE OR ADVERB?

Exercise A

1. adverb
2. adjective
3. adverb
4. adjective
5. adverb
6. adjective
7. adverb
8. adverb
9. adjective
10. adverb [or adjective]

Exercise B

(Answers will vary.)

1. usually
2. hardly
3. quickly
4. equally
5. Slowly
6. painstakingly
7. closely
8. carefully
9. happily
10. smugly

◆ WORKSHEET 15: PREPOSITIONS AND THEIR OBJECTS

Exercise A

1. for the North Pole; for many years
2. with him; on every expedition; except the first one
3. for a long time; for his role
4. as a servant; on a trip; to Nicaragua
5. with sailing
6. As a result
7. during their travels
8. On the final push; to the North Pole; with Peary
9. of the expedition; for the discovery
10. after many years; by Congress, Maryland's state government, and two U.S. presidents

Exercise B

1. Below—preposition; along—adverb
2. Next—adverb; above—preposition

◆ WORKSHEET 16: CONJUNCTIONS

Exercise A

1. but; I want to see Los Lobos in concert, but I have no money
2. not only . . . but also; not only newspapers but also aluminum cans
3. and; chopsticks and rice bowls
4. either . . . or; either Whitney Houston or Janet Jackson
5. neither . . . nor; neither too many adjectives nor too few
6. for; That diet is dangerous, for it does not meet the body's needs
7. Both . . . and; Both the Mohawk and the Oneida
8. yet; It rained all day, yet we enjoyed the trip
9. or; walk home or take the bus
10. and; Revise your paper, and proofread it carefully

Exercise B

(Answers will vary.)

1. both . . . and
2. Either . . . or

◆ WORKSHEET 17: INTERJECTIONS

Exercise A

1. Ouch
2. Oh
3. Help
4. Well
5. Wow
6. Eureka
7. Gee
8. Hooray
9. Oops
10. Shucks

Exercise B

(Sentences will vary.)

1. Whoa! This is harder than it looks.
2. Wow! You are really good at this.
3. Oh, so that's how you do it.
4. Darn! I missed the jump.
5. Yes! I got him this time!

◆ WORKSHEET 18: DETERMINING PARTS OF SPEECH

Exercise A

1. Oh—INT; just—ADV; white—ADJ
2. Did—V; or—CON; write—V
3. prepared—V; under—PREP; shelter—N
4. They—P; yet—CON; not—ADV

Exercise B

(Sentences will vary.)

1. Don't walk on the grass.—verb
   The walk helped her headache.—noun
2. That smells like spaghetti.—preposition
   I like fresh vegetables.—verb
3. I'm staying inside.—adverb
   He keeps his marbles inside a jar.—preposition
4. Who needs a fast car?—adjective
   He drives too fast.—adverb

◆ WORKSHEET 19: REVIEW

Exercise A

1. Evanti—P; woman—C; opera—C; world—C
2. age—C; four—C; concert—C; Washington, D.C.—P
3. adult—C; concert—C; White House—P; President Franklin Roosevelt—P; wife—C; Eleanor Roosevelt—P
4. career—C; singers—C

Exercise B

1. I—P; myself—I
2. something—IND; these—DEM
3. We—P; himself—R
4. Who—INT
5. who—REL

Exercise C

1. preposition—boat	6. preposition—hand
2. adverb	7. adverb
3. preposition—sailors	8. adverb
4. adverb	9. adverb
5. preposition—bluff	10. preposition—island

Exercise D

1. presents—action verb
2. has become—linking verb
3. are—linking verb; seem—linking verb
4. has—action verb; performs—action verb; speaks—action verb
5. can enjoy—action verb

Exercise E

1. ADJ; P	3. ADJ; ADV	5. CON; PREP
2. V; N	4. ADV; CON	

Chapter 2: Agreement

◆ WORKSHEET 1: SINGULAR AND PLURAL

Exercise A

1. S	5. P	9. S	13. S	17. P
2. P	6. P	10. P	14. P	18. P
3. P	7. P	11. P	15. S	19. S
4. S	8. P	12. S	16. P	20. S

Exercise B

1. S	3. S	5. S	7. P	9. P
2. S	4. P	6. S	8. S	10. P

◆ WORKSHEET 2: AGREEMENT OF SUBJECT AND VERB A

Exercise A

1. seem	3. tell	5. was
2. writes	4. has	

Exercise B: Proofreading

1. has	3. C	5. C
2. stands	4. are	

◆ WORKSHEET 3: AGREEMENT OF SUBJECT AND VERB B

Exercise A

1. history; begins	6. author; is
2. New York; was	7. writers; include
3. governor; was	8. winner; was
4. immigrants; have	9. writer; is
5. names; are	10. contributions; enrich

Exercise B: Proofreading

1. tidal wave; C	4. force; causes
2. eruption; C	5. Walls; are
3. network; alerts	

◆ WORKSHEET 4: AGREEMENT WITH INDEFINITE PRONOUNS

Exercise A

1. Neither; was	4. Each; studies
2. Everybody; gets	5. No one; was
3. Someone; donates	

Exercise B

1. occur	3. are	5. are
2. understand	4. make	

◆ WORKSHEET 5: AGREEMENT WITH COMPOUND SUBJECTS

Exercise A

1. S—was	3. P—rent	5. S—was
2. P—are	4. P—need	

Exercise B

1. are	3. is	5. are
2. is	4. shows	

◆ WORKSHEET 6: OTHER PROBLEMS IN AGREEMENT A

Exercise

1. solutions; are	6. passion; is
2. team; were	7. notes; are
3. both; Are	8. candidates; were
4. members; come	9. family; has
5. puppies; are	10. masks; are

◆ WORKSHEET 7: OTHER PROBLEMS IN AGREEMENT B

Exercise A

1. is	3. Here are	5. has
2. seems	4. are	

Exercise B

1. Doesn't	3. doesn't	5. don't
2. don't	4. Don't	

◆ **WORKSHEET 8: AGREEMENT OF PRONOUN AND ANTECEDENT**

Exercise

Pronoun	Antecedent
1. his or her	writer
2. they	Paula, Eric
3. he	Mark, Hector
4. his or her	One
5. its	Each
6. their	sister, boyfriend
7. his or her	Everyone
8. his or her	Neither
9. he or she	Anyone
10. her	Kat, Liz

◆ **WORKSHEET 9: REVIEW**

Exercise A: Revising

1. There surely are few teenage artists as successful as Yani.

2. In fact, the People's Republic of China regards her as a national treasure.

3. C

4. A painter since the age of two, Yani doesn't paint in just one style.

5. Her ideas and her art naturally change over the years.

6. Several paintings show one of Yani's favorite childhood subjects.

7. Many of her early paintings feature monkeys.

8. In fact, one of her large works pictures 112 monkeys.

9. However, most of her later paintings are of landscapes, other animals, and people.

10. Yani fills her paintings with energy and life.

Exercise B

1. is	5. work	9. is
2. prefers	6. are	10. was
3. enjoy	7. come	
4. doesn't	8. is	

Exercise C

(The first item in each pair is the incorrect usage in the sentence. The second item is the corrected usage.)

1. their—his or her	6. C
2. his or her—their	7. their—her
3. his—their	8. he or she—they
4. their—his	9. their—his or her
5. their—his or her	10. their—its

Chapter 3: Using Verbs

◆ **WORKSHEET 1: REGULAR VERBS**

Exercise

1. practiced	3. wanted	5. promised
2. perform	4. used	6. leaned

7. starting	9. danced
8. requested	10. filled

◆ **WORKSHEET 2: IRREGULAR VERBS**

Exercise

1. blew	6. came	11. gone	16. shrank
2. kept	7. done	12. known	17. spoken
3. brought	8. drank	13. rang	18. thrown
4. burst	9. fallen	14. ran	19. written
5. chose	10. frozen	15. saw	20. swam

◆ **WORKSHEET 3: VERB TENSE**

Exercise: Proofreading

Present	Past
1. strikes; run	struck; ran
2. exclaim	exclaimed
3. has gone	had gone
4. light; play	lighted *or* lit; played
5. know; has hit; keeps	knew; had hit; kept
6. asks; is	asked; is
7. is; tell	is; told
8. nods	nodded
9. start; does understand; am talking; walks	started; did understand was talking; walked
10. are; shines; works	were; shone; worked

◆ **WORKSHEET 4: COMMONLY CONFUSED VERBS**

Exercise

1. lain	5. sat	9. sitting
2. Sit	6. lay	10. risen
3. laid	7. rose	
4. lying	8. set	

◆ **WORKSHEET 5: REVIEW**

Exercise A

1. sits—present	4. destroyed—past
2. tells—present	5. will read—future
3. suffered—past	

Exercise B

1. wrote	5. made	9. knew
2. come	6. built	10. did
3. stood	7. drew	
4. seen	8. taken	

Exercise C: Proofreading

(The first item in each pair is the incorrect usage in the sentence. The second item is the corrected usage.)

1. builded—built	6. growed—grew
2. went—gone	7. raised—rose
3. lays—lies	8. set—sat
4. use—used	9. spoke—spoken
5. maked—made	10. C

Exercise D: Revising

1. By the time the frontier closed in 1890, thousands of hardy pioneers had traveled across the country in Conestoga wagons.

2. After the president of the United States threw out the first ball, the baseball game began. *or* After the President of the United States throws out the first ball, the baseball game begins.

3. The hungry traveler will eat some crackers and drink a cup of milk. *or* The hungry traveler ate some crackers and drank a cup of milk.

4. Eduardo was working in the garden when he heard the strange sound. *or* Eduardo is working in the garden when he hears the strange sound.

Chapter 4: Using Pronouns

◆ WORKSHEET 1: CASE FORMS

Exercise A
1. O   2. P   3. N   4. O   5. P

Exercise B
1. P   2. N   3. O   4. N   5. O

◆ WORKSHEET 2: NOMINATIVE CASE

Exercise A
1. I   3. he and I   5. We
2. he and I   4. I

Exercise B: Proofreading
(The first item in each pair is the incorrect usage in the sentence. The second item is the corrected usage.)
1. C   3. her—she   5. us—we
2. him—he   4. him—he

◆ WORKSHEET 3: OBJECTIVE CASE A

Exercise
(Pronouns will vary.)
1. him—DO
2. him—IO; us—IO
3. her—IO
4. her—DO; them—DO
5. them—IO
6. us—DO
7. her—IO; me—IO
8. her—DO; him—DO
9. me—DO
10. him—IO

◆ WORKSHEET 4: OBJECTIVE CASE B

Exercise
1. her
2. them
3. him
4. her
5. her
6. them
7. him
8. her
9. him
10. her

◆ WORKSHEET 5: *WHO* AND *WHOM*

Exercise A
1. Who   3. whom   5. whom
2. Whom   4. whom

Exercise B
1. Who   3. Whom   5. who; whom
2. whom   4. Who

◆ WORKSHEET 6: OTHER PRONOUN PROBLEMS

Exercise A
1. us   3. We   5. us
2. we   4. we

Exercise B: Proofreading
(The first item in each pair is the incorrect usage in the sentence. The second item is the corrected usage.)
1. himself—he   4. C
2. hisself—himself   5. themselves—they
3. myself—I

◆ WORKSHEET 7: REVIEW

Exercise A
1. me—IO   5. them—OP   9. them—IO
2. her—IO   6. her—DO   10. them—OP
3. him—OP   7. she—PN
4. I—S   8. we—S

Exercise B
1. he
2. him
3. them
4. I
5. they
6. he
7. him and me
8. he
9. her and them
10. me
11. us
12. I
13. she
14. me
15. himself
16. he and she
17. themselves
18. him and me
19. We
20. Whom

Exercise C: Proofreading
(The first item in each pair is the incorrect usage in the sentence. The second item is the corrected usage.)
1. him—he
2. hisself—himself
3. C
4. them and him—they and he
5. herself—her
6. C
7. he—him
8. him—he
9. hisself—himself
10. we—us

Chapter 5: Using Modifiers

◆ WORKSHEET 1: DEGREES OF COMPARISON

Exercise
1. C—2   5. P—1   9. S—3 or more
2. S—3 or more   6. P—1   10. S—3 or more
3. S—3 or more   7. C—2
4. C—2   8. C—2

◆ WORKSHEET 2: REGULAR COMPARISON

Exercise

(Note: Students may show decreasing comparisons, using less and least.)

Comparative	Superlative
1. nearer	nearest
2. greater	greatest
3. more carefully	most carefully
4. more honestly	most honestly
5. smaller	smallest
6. tinier	tiniest
7. more timidly	most timidly
8. more enthusiastically	most enthusiastically
9. safer	safest
10. shadier	shadiest

◆ WORKSHEET 3: USES OF COMPARATIVE AND SUPERLATIVE FORMS

Exercise

1. bigger	6. most mysterious
2. prettier	7. famous *or* most famous
3. freshest	8. most interesting
4. easier	9. more slowly
5. livelier	10. greater

◆ WORKSHEET 4: IRREGULAR COMPARISON

Exercise A

1. better	5. more	9. best
2. best	6. most	10. worst
3. More	7. worse	
4. best	8. farther	

Exercise B

(Answers will vary.)

1. good	3. best	5. better
2. farthest	4. well	

◆ WORKSHEET 5: DOUBLE COMPARISON AND DOUBLE NEGATIVE

Exercise A: Proofreading

(The first item in each pair is the incorrect usage in the sentence. The second item is the corrected usage.)

1. more rainier—rainier	3. more longer—longer
2. most saddest—saddest	4. more stronger—stronger

Exercise B: Revising

1. I didn't see anyone [*or* I saw no one] I knew at the game.

2. Early explorers searched that area of Florida for gold, but they didn't find any [*or* they found none].

3. We could hardly hear the guest speaker.

4. Double negatives have no place [*or* don't have any place] in standard English.

◆ WORKSHEET 6: MISPLACED PREPOSITIONAL PHRASES

Exercise: Revising

(Answers may vary.)

1. That woman in high heels and a tweed suit was out walking her dog this morning.

2. I knew I'd need a bicycle by the end of the year.

3. Hoy taught us how to eat rice with chopsticks.

4. On Monday our teacher said the class would put on a play.

5. Don't forget to take the box with the empty bottles to the store.

◆ WORKSHEET 7: MISPLACED AND DANGLING PARTICIPIAL PHRASES

Exercise: Revising

(Answers may vary.)

1. I watched the lion pacing around its kill.

2. The circus featured a clown wearing a bright orange suit and floppy yellow shoes.

3. The girls walked through the field filled with daisies.

4. Stuffed with sage and bread crumbs, the turkey was large enough for three families.

5. Tired from the long walk through the snow, the travelers welcomed food and rest.

◆ WORKSHEET 8: MISPLACED ADJECTIVE CLAUSES

Exercise A

1. *Cujo* which was made into a movie

2. King whom my friend admires

3. stories which are true classics and horrifying enough for anyone

4. story that is about the sound of a heartbeat

5. Mary Shelley whose novel *Frankenstein* has terrified readers for more than a hundred years

Exercise B: Revising

1. The students who made the first presentation received an A.

2. The kitten that is in the tree belongs to my neighbor.

3. My friend Beverly, who lives in Sarasota, Florida, visited me.

4. The doctor who examined them said that the triplets were healthy.

5. The picnic that we had in the park was fun.

◆ WORKSHEET 9: REVIEW

Exercise A

(Note: Students may show decreasing comparisons, using less and least.)

Comparative	Superlative
1. farther	farthest
2. more	most
3. more terrific	most terrific
4. riper	ripest

5. more silently   most silently
6. younger   youngest
7. more marvelous   most marvelous
8. shadier   shadiest
9. more gently   most gently
10. stronger   strongest

Exercise B: Revising

(Answers may vary.)

1. Kendo, a Japanese martial art, is more graceful than many other sports.

2. Sylvia Yee plays chess better than anyone else her age.

3. Time hardly moves during the summer.

4. Which of the twins is stronger?

5. Some people don't seem to have any control over their tempers.

Exercise C: Revising

(Answers may vary.)

1. The waiter brought plates piled high with spaghetti and sauce to Terrell and me.

2. The stranger was frightened by the dogs barking and growling.

3. On Friday he said no one had applied for the job.

4. The house that my parents want to buy is about a mile from Dunbar High School.

5. Trees all over the city are covered with pecans at this time of year.

Exercise D: Revising

(Answers may vary.)

1. Born with Down's syndrome, Chris is the youngest of four children.

2. On the show he played a character whose name is Corky.

3. Chris certainly is one of the best actors that I've seen.

4. Chris doesn't ever seem nervous about being a TV star.

5. Chris, who says he has "Up syndrome," usually has a positive attitude.

Chapter 6: Phrases

◆ WORKSHEET 1: PREPOSITIONAL PHRASES

Exercise A

1. of these soldiers

2. in Vietnam

3. for a memorial; to the Vietnam veterans *(Students are not asked at this point to make this distinction, but some students may recognize that the prepositional phrase* to the Vietnam veterans *is part of the larger phrase* for a memorial to the Vietnam veterans.)

4. of all American soldiers *(Although they are not asked here to include modifiers that follow the object of the preposition, some students may recognize that the adjective clause* who had died or were missing *is part of the prepositional phrase.)*

5. of great effort

6. to the project

7. in Washington, D.C.

8. from Lin's design

9. from Memphis, Tennessee; on the shiny granite

10. in Vietnam; by the people; of the United States *(Students are not asked at this point to make this distinction, but some students may recognize that the prepositional phrase* of the United States *is part of the larger phrase* by the people of the United States.)

Exercise B

(Answers will vary.)

1. with a yellow racing stripe

2. In the alley

3. next to Mr. Alvarez

4. under the table

5. In the attic

◆ WORKSHEET 2: ADJECTIVE PHRASES

Exercise A

1. about a rich man's repentance

2. with wealth and property

3. of miserable poverty

4. from the past, present, and future

5. of them

Exercise B

1. friends with Pierre Curie

2. fame as a scientist

3. two of them

4. enthusiasm for science

5. marriage between the two lovers; lovers of science *(Although they are not asked to make this distinction, some students may recognize that the prepositional phrase* of science *is actually part of the larger phrase* between the two lovers of science.)

◆ WORKSHEET 3: ADVERB PHRASES

Exercise

1. into the Pecos River—fell

2. for him—searched

3. by coyotes—was saved

4. for many years—thought

5. After a long argument—convinced

6. During a drought—dug

7. On one occasion—rode

8. from a ledge—leaped

9. for trouble—ready

10. in the West—common

◆ WORKSHEET 4: PARTICIPLES AND PARTICIPIAL PHRASES

Exercise

1. journals written in reverse mirror writing

2. pictures showing birds in flight

3. machines based on his sketches of birds in flight

4. first recorded in history

5. Studying the eye Leonardo

6. He filling his journals with sketches

7. solutions reached in his journals

8. hands sketched in the journals

9. Painting on a large wall Leonardo

10. Leonardo experimenting continually

◆ WORKSHEET 5: INFINITIVES AND INFINITIVE PHRASES

Exercise A

1. to visit   3. to symbolize   5. to express

2. to see   4. none

Exercise B

1. to control each of its feathers

2. to push their bodies through the air

3. to build aircraft

4. to claim its territory

5. To recognize the songs of different birds

◆ WORKSHEET 6: REVIEW

Exercise A

1. of types—ADJ—hundreds

2. into twenty-eight large families—ADV—group

3. within the same family—ADJ—Sharks

4. among families—ADJ—differences

5. throughout the world's oceans—ADV—are found

Exercise B

1. read in our synagogue—PART

2. Celebrated in September or October—PART

3. to wear white robes instead of the usual black robes—INF

4. Representing newness and purity—PART

5. baked by my grandmother—PART

6. knowing that Yom Kippur, a day of fasting, is only ten days away—PART

7. considered the holiest day of the Jewish year—PART

8. To attend services—INF

9. to see many neighbors there—INF

10. marking the day's end—PART

Chapter 7: Clauses

◆ WORKSHEET 1: INDEPENDENT CLAUSES

Exercise A

1. Can you name

2. performers had

3. Berry Gordy began

4. he could spot

5. Gordy went

6. The Miracles had

7. Robinson was

8. Gordy managed

9. Diana Ross and the Supremes, Stevie Wonder, Marvin Gaye, The Four Tops, The Temptations, Gladys Knight and the Pips, Michael Jackson are

10. can you remember

Exercise B

(Answers will vary.)

1. When I graduate from high school, I hope to go to college.

2. If you want to read a good book, you should try *King of the Wind.*

◆ WORKSHEET 2: SUBORDINATE CLAUSES

Exercise A

1. that is coated with a shiny substance

2. which is flat

3. that is reflected in a plane mirror

4. As you look into a mirror

5. When an image is reversed

6. who looks through a periscope

7. which show a wide area of the road behind

8. because convex mirrors make reflected objects appear far away

9. Because the mirror in a flashlight is concave, or curved inward

10. When you look in a concave mirror

Exercise B

(Answers will vary.)

1. I bought the CD that I've wanted for a long time.

2. My parents have agreed to let us go if we call when we get there.

◆ WORKSHEET 3: THE ADJECTIVE CLAUSE

Exercise A

1. In his later years, Jefferson lived at (Monticello), which he had designed.

2. Jefferson planned a daily (schedule) that kept him busy all day.

3. He began each day by making a (note) that recorded the morning temperature.

4. Then he did his (writing), which included letters to friends and businesspersons.

5. Afterward, he ate (breakfast), which was served around 9:00 A.M.

Exercise B

(Answers will vary.)

1. You should proofread every composition that you hand in.

2. We heard a sound that startled us.

3. Ramón wrote the song that we sang in the contest.

4. Then she told the joke that Sara had told earlier.

5. There is the dog that I want.

◆ WORKSHEET 4: THE ADVERB CLAUSE

Exercise

1. when they were about to be attacked by an enemy—when

2. As one of the emperor's advisers was thinking—when

3. so that they might be used to frighten the enemy—why

4. so that the enemy would hear the kites but not see them—why

5. as if they were being chased by a fire-breathing dragon—how

◆ WORKSHEET 5: REVIEW

Exercise A

1. SUB—that was assigned
2. SUB—bicycle was
3. SUB—who lost
4. SUB—package arrives
5. IND—Did you read
6. SUB—weather is
7. SUB—they performed
8. IND—William Shakespeare is
9. SUB—you would like
10. IND—(you) help

Exercise B

1. What costume did you wear to the party that Juanita had?
2. My costume, which won a prize, was a chicken suit!
3. My cousin, whom I took to the party, went as a huge mosquito.
4. I couldn't recognize many of the people who were in costume.
5. Did you recognize Hillary, who came as a gorilla?
6. The person whom I didn't recognize was Mingan.
7. His costume, which was really original, was a large cardboard box.
8. The box, which was covered with clear plastic, was very shiny.
9. Mingan, who was hidden inside the box, kept saying, "I'm melting!"
10. The box that he wore was supposed to be an ice cube!

Exercise C

1. As soon as the ground softens in the spring—when
2. than others do—how much
3. If you want to grow morning glories—under what condition
4. When the seeds sprout—when
5. so that the plants can climb—why
6. After the young plants grow strong—when
7. as if they are big blue trumpets—how
8. because they open each morning—why
9. When they are warmed by the morning sun—when
10. If the day is dark or stormy—under what condition

Exercise D

1. When you study the Revolutionary War—adverb clause
2. whose real name is believed to have been Mary Ludwig—adjective clause
3. Although she was born in New Jersey—adverb clause
4. who was a barber—adjective clause
5. when the Revolution began—adverb clause
6. which was the site of a battle on a hot June day in 1778—adjective clause
7. so that they would not be overcome by the intense heat—adverb clause
8. because she carried the water in pitchers—adverb clause
9. when her husband collapsed from the heat—adverb clause
10. who was the commander of the Continental Army—adjective clause

Chapter 8: Sentences

◆ WORKSHEET 1: SENTENCES AND SENTENCE FRAGMENTS

Exercise: Revising
(Revisions will vary.)

1. S
2. F—She enjoyed running the rapids.
3. S
4. F—She got a shock when the river dropped suddenly.
5. F—The river went around a bend and became foaming rapids full of dangerous boulders.
6. F—They were huge granite boulders, which can break a boat.
7. S
8. F—My aunt made the trip with one guide and four passengers.
9. S
10. F—These boats are capable of carrying eighteen passengers.

◆ WORKSHEET 2: SUBJECT AND PREDICATE

Exercise A
(Answers will vary.)

1. Soccer is a difficult game to play.
2. Jack works in the post office.
3. Luckily for me, this book was easy to read.
4. Tied to the end of the dock was a rowboat.
5. Did anyone help you?

Exercise B
(Answers will vary.)

1. My favorite food is spinach.
2. A course in first aid is offered here.
3. Has our car been repaired?

4. Rock climbing is fun.

5. Spanish explorers in the Americas were looking for gold.

6. Several computers were given to our school.

7. In the box was a new pair of roller skates.

8. The skyscrapers of New York City loomed above us.

9. Some dogs chase cars.

10. Has my family arrived yet?

◆ WORKSHEET 3:   COMPLETE SUBJECT AND SIMPLE SUBJECT

Exercise

1. Ray Bradbury

2. *The Golden Apples of the Sun*

3. My favorite story in that book

4. The main character in the story

5. Mr. Eckels

6. He

7. Bradbury's hero

8. Trouble

9. the past

10. The results of that mistake

◆ WORKSHEET 4:   COMPLETE PREDICATE AND SIMPLE PREDICATE

Exercise

1. are unsure about the history of the Stars and Stripes

2. approved a design for the flag

3. included thirteen red stripes and thirteen white stripes

4. was a blue field with thirteen white stars

5. remains a mystery

6. During the Revolutionary War, needed a symbol of their independence

7. wanted flags for the army

8. Unfortunately, did not arrive until after the Revolutionary War

9. According to legend, made the first flag

10. doubt the Betsy Ross story

◆ WORKSHEET 5:   THE VERB PHRASE

Exercise A

1. is called

2. was settled

3. have contributed

4. has

5. may be viewed

Exercise B

1. had built

2. have seen

3. could have been sleeping

4. might be

5. Does have

◆ WORKSHEET 6:   COMPOUND SUBJECTS AND COMPOUND VERBS

Exercise A

1. parks, monuments

2. Grand Canyon, waterfalls

3. Water, forces

4. bridges, arches

5. Skyline Arch, Landscape Arch

Exercise B

1. Have heard, learned

2. found, carved

3. placed, began

4. used, threw

5. took, competed

◆ WORKSHEET 7:   REVIEW

Exercise A

1. F	3. F	5. S	7. F	9. F
2. S	4. F	6. S	8. F	10. S

Exercise B

(Answers will vary.)

1. Algebra I is the hardest course I have this semester.

2. Every morning before school, I deliver newspapers.

3. Does her best friend know about the party?

4. Found behind the counter was a box of money.

5. By the end of the day, Jorge is tired.

6. Marcia and Elena brought the dessert.

7. At my house politics is the one thing we all agree on.

8. Over the fence went the ball.

9. Can you help me?

10. The books on that cart should be returned to the shelves.

Exercise C

1. Momaday was born, lived

2. father was

3. Momaday enrolled, attended

4. Momaday tells

5. Included are poems, essay, stories

6. *The Way to Rainy Mountain* was published

7. Have you read

8. William Least Heat-Moon traveled, wrote

9. Did travels inspire

10. Readers enjoy

Exercise D

1. Settlers faced, overcame

2. Mount McKinley, Mount Whitney are

3. Everglades protects

4. skiers rush

5. stars have been born, raised

6. valleys, forests cool, refresh

7. campgrounds, overlooks provide

8. Mount Evans is, can be reached

9. view is

10. name comes, means

Chapter 9: Complements

◆ WORKSHEET 1: RECOGNIZING COMPLEMENTS

Exercise A

Subject	Verb	Complement
1. computer	saved	document
2. He	chose	shirt
3. bus	passed	me
4. Laurette	won	
5. sister	Is	veterinarian

Exercise B

(Answers will vary.)

1. Winter is my favorite season.
2. Everyone gave the teacher a report.

◆ WORKSHEET 2: DIRECT OBJECTS

Exercise A

1. T—glass   3. L   5. T—sacks
2. T—poem   4. L

Exercise B

1. strength, endurance   4. pounds
2. miles   5. swimmers
3. grease

◆ WORKSHEET 3: INDIRECT OBJECTS

Exercise

1. us, seats   6. us, words
2. you, typewriter   7. horse, hay
3. Octavio Paz, Nobel Prize   8. me, card
4. me, moccasins   9. you, apology
5. children, stories   10. Ricardo, seat

◆ WORKSHEET 4: PREDICATE NOMINATIVES AND PREDICATE ADJECTIVES

Exercise

1. is—mountain—PN
2. felt—good—PA
3. smells—sour—PA
4. remains—choice—PN
5. will be—president—PN
6. became—Thailand—PN
7. taste—delicious—PA
8. can be—problem—PN
9. appears—complicated—PA
10. remained—calm—PA

◆ WORKSHEET 5: REVIEW

Exercise A

1. them—indirect object; answer—direct object
2. article—direct object
3. days—direct object

4. people, land—direct object
5. reservation—direct object
6. mountains, Flathead Lake—direct object
7. me—indirect object; jobs—direct object
8. father—indirect object; directions—direct object
9. Standing Arrow Pow-Wow—direct object
10. visitors—indirect object; dances, games—direct object

Exercise B

1. pianist—predicate nominative
2. green—predicate adjective
3. happy—predicate adjective
4. spice—predicate nominative
5. lawyer—predicate nominative
6. name—predicate nominative
7. thoughtful—predicate adjective
8. state—predicate nominative
9. cheerful—predicate adjective
10. loud—predicate adjective

Exercise C

1. scout—PN
2. woodcrafter, trapper—PN
3. tales—DO
4. generations—IO; hero—DO
5. emergency—DO
6. faithful, fearless—PA
7. forest, country—DO
8. miserable—PA
9. him—DO
10. no one—IO; views—DO

Chapter 10: Kinds of Sentences

◆ WORKSHEET 1: SIMPLE SENTENCES

Exercise

1. escape—S; is—V
2. woods, activities—S; are—V
3. size—S; can be—V
4. I—S; take—V
5. I—S; can find—V
6. brothers, I—S; row, climb, have—V
7. I—S; watch, wander—V
8. pair—S; followed—V
9. birds—S; got, flew—V
10. family, I—S; can enjoy—V

◆ WORKSHEET 2: COMPOUND SENTENCES

Exercise

Subject	Verb	Type
1. Amazon River	is located, is	simple
2. Amazon	begins	
it	flows	compound

3. river	carries, drains	simple
4. Amazon	is	
people	think	compound
5. rivers	drain	
river	overflows	compound

◆ WORKSHEET 3: COMPLEX SENTENCES

Exercise

1. who is famous throughout the world—who

2. After she recovered from the illness—After

3. Because she could not hear—Because

4. who trained teachers of people with hearing impairments—who

5. whose name was Anne Sullivan—whose

6. as the child touched the object represented by the word—as

7. which is the alphabet used by people with visual impairments—which

8. who had been partly cured of blindness herself—who

9. Because she had triumphed over her disabilities—Because

10. which is entitled *The Story of My Life*—which

◆ WORKSHEET 4: CLASSIFYING SENTENCES BY PURPOSE

Exercise

1. . . . Johnson.—DEC	6. . . . answered?—INT
2. . . . is!—EXC	7. . . . mind.—IMP
3. . . . men.—IMP	8. . . . assassination.—DEC
4. . . . conspiracy?—INT	9. . . . them!—EXC
5. . . . deaths.—DEC	10. . . . again. (*or* !)—IMP

◆ WORKSHEET 5: REVIEW

Exercise A

1. S	3. CD	5. CD
2. CD	4. S	

Exercise B

1. CX	3. CX	5. CX
2. CD	4. CD	

Exercise C

1. complex	5. complex	9. simple
2. complex	6. compound	10. complex
3. compound	7. simple	
4. simple	8. complex	

Exercise D

1. . . . prairie.—DEC	6. . . . are!—EXC
2. . . . burrows.—DEC	7. . . . community.—DEC
3. . . . acres.—DEC	8. . . . better.—IMP
4. . . . prairie dog?—INT	9. . . . danger.—DEC
5. . . . morning.—DEC	10. . . . colony.—DEC

Chapter 11: Writing Effective Sentences

◆ WORKSHEET 1: SENTENCE FRAGMENTS

Exercise A

1. F	3. F	5. F	7. S	9. F
2. F	4. S	6. F	8. F	10. S

Exercise B: Revising

(*Answers will vary.*)

1. The whole family got into the car.

2. When we arrived at the campground, we unpacked.

◆ WORKSHEET 2: RUN-ON SENTENCES

Exercise: Revising

(*Revisions may vary.*)

1. Saturn is a huge planet. It is almost ten times the size of Earth.

2. Saturn is covered by clouds, and it is circled by bands of color.

3. Sometimes the clouds at the equator appear yellow, but the clouds at the poles appear green.

4. Saturn has at least eighteen moons. Titan is the largest moon.

5. Saturn rotates faster than Earth does, and its day is only 10 ½ hours long.

6. C

7. Saturn has seven rings. They spread out far from the planet.

8. C

9. C

10. Saturn is a beautiful planet. You need a telescope to see its rings.

◆ WORKSHEET 3: COMBINING SENTENCES BY INSERTING WORDS AND PHRASES

Exercise: Revising

(*Answers may vary.*)

1. Henry David Thoreau was a thoughtful individualist.

2. Thoreau lived near a peaceful pond in Massachusetts.

3. In the spring of 1845, Thoreau built a home near Walden Pond.

4. First, he dug a cellar in the sandy soil.

5. He cut the timbers from tall white pines.

6. His friends came to help him set up the framework.

7. Thoreau kept his weekly grocery bill to twenty-seven cents by growing most of his food.

8. He would lie under a beech tree to rest from his writing.

9. Thoreau loved the smooth, clear, deep pond.

10. Lying on its frozen surface, he measured its depth.

◆ WORKSHEET 4: COMBINING BY USING *AND*, *BUT*, OR *OR*

Exercise A: Revising

(Answers may vary.)

1. Dolphins can't smell or taste things as people do.

2. Baby dolphins catch and ride waves near the beach.

3. Sharks sometimes attack and kill porpoises.

4. A porpoise or a tuna could outswim most sharks.

Exercise B: Revising

1. Some Pueblo peoples have lived in the same area for generations, and they have strong ties to their land.

2. Many Pueblo people live in the Southwest, and [*or* but] some live in other parts of the country.

3. Some Pueblo land is desert, but the people can grow crops if they irrigate.

4. The traditional adobe homes have several stories, and sometimes ladders are used to reach the upper levels.

◆ WORKSHEET 5: COMBINING BY USING A SUBORDINATE CLAUSE

Exercise: Revising

(Answers may vary.)

1. The pearl is a gem that is made by certain kinds of oysters and clams.

2. Beautiful pearls are found in tropical seas, where the best pearl oysters live.

3. A valuable pearl has a shine that comes from below its surface.

4. A pearl becomes round when it is formed in the soft part of the oyster.

5. Pearls should be wiped clean with a soft cloth after they are worn as jewelry.

◆ WORKSHEET 6: STRINGY SENTENCES AND WORDY SENTENCES

Exercise A: Revising

(Answers may vary.)

1. After working as a nurse, she joined the Women's Army Corps. She soon became an officer.

2. C

3. When the war ended, she was promoted to captain. Later her official rank rose to major.

4. During the Korean War, she worked as an intelligence officer, studying information about the enemy.

Exercise B: Revising

(Answers may vary.)

1. Starfish are fascinating creatures.

2. A starfish has little feet tipped with powerful suction cups.

3. C

4. Although the eyespot cannot see things, it can tell light from dark.

◆ WORKSHEET 7: REVIEW

Exercise A: Revising

(Answers may vary.)

Many plants can survive where the climate is hot and dry. Cacti, Joshua trees, palm trees, and wildflowers grow in deserts. These plants do not grow close together. Because they are spread out, each plant gets water and minerals from a large area.

Exercise B: Revising

1. Peanuts are a major crop grown in many warm regions.

2. Peanuts are a healthful food for snacking.

3. The oil from peanuts is used in many dressings for salads.

4. Low grades of peanut oil are used to make soap.

Exercise C: Revising

(Answers may vary.)

Athena, the goddess of wisdom, caught and tamed Pegasus. Only a hero or a true poet could ride Pegasus. The first person to ride the winged horse was a Greek youth named Bellerophon, who was sent by a king to kill a monster. Bellerophon destroyed the monster and became a hero.

Exercise D: Revising

(Answers may vary.)

The puppets used in *The Dark Crystal* were different from the original Muppets. They weren't as brightly colored as the TV Muppets. They also had legs and could move through a scene with their whole bodies showing. Some of the characters in *The Dark Crystal* were radio-controlled. Others were operated by puppeteers who were hidden under the movie set.

Chapter 12: Capital Letters

◆ WORKSHEET 1: USING CAPITAL LETTERS A

Exercise: Proofreading

1. (L)ast year (I) went to live with my aunt and uncle.

2. (T)hey love to read and asked me, "(W)hat are your favorite books?"

3. (I) had never read very much, so (I) said, '(I) don't know yet."

4. (W)e started reading aloud to one another every evening.

5. (W)e read poetry by many poets, and oh, (I) loved it all.

6. Edgar Allan Poe's "Annabel Lee" starts, "(I)t was many and many a year ago. . . ."

7. (M)y aunt would say, "(W)hat shall we read tonight, (O) literate one?"

8. (L)ater my uncle said, '(L)et's read some of Robert Louis Stevenson's novels."

9. we did, and then we read Sandra Cisneros, James Thurber, and Jamaica Kincaid.

10. if you asked me "what are your favorite books?" i still would say "i don't know"; but now it's because i have too many favorites!

◆ WORKSHEET 2:   USING CAPITAL LETTERS B

Exercise: Proofreading

1. My family, including our dog rover, was lucky enough to watch the Moon rise over hawaii on the fourth of july last year.

2. The Hawaiian islands are located in the pacific ocean, nearly 2,400 miles West of san francisco, california.

3. Hawaii became the fiftieth State in the united states in 1959.

4. Our teacher, Ms. castillo, explained that the capital City is honolulu and that it is located on the southeast Coast of oahu.

5. hawaii volcanoes national park is on hawaii, the largest island.

◆ WORKSHEET 3:   USING CAPITAL LETTERS C

Exercise: Proofreading

the branford mall is the largest in melville county. it is on jefferson parkway, two miles north of duck lake state park. across the parkway from the mall is the new branford high school, home of the branford panthers. near the mall are the american legion hall, bowlorama, and the beautiful new first methodist church.

the mall has two jewelry stores, nicholson's department store, the palace cinema, and thirty-five other businesses, including a restaurant owned by jean larue from france, who last year won the best chef in the midwest award. the mall also has an outlet store for northwestern boating goods of chicago. for memorial day a scale model of the uss arizona was displayed with pictures of local people who fought in world war II.

◆ WORKSHEET 4:   USING CAPITAL LETTERS D

Exercise

1. Russian, Hungarian, Polish
2. European
3. Scandinavian, Norway, Sweden
4. Australian
5. English, Elizabethan Age
6. Computer I
7. Persian, Ethiopian
8. England, France, Scotland, Russia, United States, Canadian

9. Chinese, Japanese
10. Indian, Greek

◆ WORKSHEET 5:   USING CAPITAL LETTERS E

Exercise: Proofreading

(Optional capitalization is underscored.)

1. While waiting to interview mayor ward, I read an article in newsweek.

2. Have you read leslie marmon silko's poem "story from bear country"?

3. Here is a picture of the thinker, one of rodin's finest sculptures.

4. On television last night we saw a movie called the three faces of eve.

5. The voters elected a president and several united states senators.

6. My uncle nick read francisco jiménez's short story "the circuit."

7. The reporter asked, "Can you tell us, general, whether you are retiring?"

8. The speaker was dr. bell, former president of the university of maine.

9. uncle don, aunt pat, aunt jean, and my grandmother were there.

10. The president met with his advisors before he spoke to the nation.

◆ WORKSHEET 6:   REVIEW

Exercise: Proofreading

1. The curtis soap corporation sponsors the television show called three is two too many.

2. the show's theme song is "you And I might get by."

3. One actor on the show is joe fontana, jr., who plays the Physician, dr. mullins.

4. The female lead, jan bledsoe, went to our junior High School here in houston, Texas.

5. The action takes place out West, just after the end of the civil war.

6. The program, which is loosely based on the book two out west, is on monday nights.

7. One episode took place at a Fourth Of July picnic, where dr. mullins approached the sheriff and said, "hey, sheriff, i challenge you to a pie-eating contest."

8. ms. Bledsoe plays a teacher who is married to mr. Reginald wildon Foster II, President of the flint bank.

9. Mrs. Foster teaches Latin, Home Economics, and History at flintsville's one-room school, and oh, does she have problems with her students!

10. One local character, uncle Ramón, once played a practical joke on Judge Grimsby right outside the mayor's office.

11. Some people, including mom, think the program is silly, but my father enjoys watching it occasionally.

12. I don't think it will win an emmy from the Academy Of Television Arts And Sciences.

13. grandma murray and aunt edna in mobile, Alabama, watch the program.

14. On monday night's show, an alien named romax and his pet zarrf [or Zarrf] from the planet zarko came to Town and stayed at the Sidewinder hotel.

15. The alien, who looked like United States president zachary taylor, spoke english perfectly and could read people's minds.

16. He settled a dispute between the Pacific Railroad Company and the flint bank.

17. On another show a united states Senator and Romax discussed their views of justice.

18. Romax said, "i don't know when you, O Earthlings, will realize that Laws must apply equally to everyone or there is no justice."

19. A week later, mayor Murdstone lost his only copy of his secret recipe for irish stew and saw the recipe in the next issue of the flintsville weekly gazette.

20. One time a mysterious buddhist priest appeared, claiming he had sailed to the east around cape horn on the ship *The Gem Of The Ocean.*

Chapter 13: Punctuation

◆ WORKSHEET 1: USING END MARKS

Exercise: Proofreading

1. . . . dance"?   6. Mrs. . . . me.
2. . . . Caribbean.   7. . . . her?
3. . . . saw.   8. . . . N.Y.
4. . . . United States. 9. . . . Award.
5. . . . person!   10. . . . barriers.

◆ WORKSHEET 2: USING COMMAS A

Exercise: Proofreading

1. Cleveland, Toledo, and Dayton are three large cities in Ohio.

2. The captain entered the cockpit, checked the instruments, and prepared for takeoff.

3. C

4. The neighbors searched behind the garages, in the bushes, and along the highway.

5. Eleanor Roosevelt's courage, her humanity, and her service to the nation will always be remembered.

6. Mrs. Ortega won more votes than Mr. Harris, Miss Steinberg, or Dr. Gladstone.

7. The chairperson's job was calling the meeting to order, asking for the minutes, and announcing new officers.

8. Todd's uncle sold an oak chest, two tables, a china lamp, and four paintings.

9. Autos, trucks, and buses were stranded by the storm.

10. The zoo director had to feed the animals, guide visitors, and keep the grounds safe and clean.

◆ WORKSHEET 3: USING COMMAS B

Exercise: Proofreading

1. Singer writes entertaining, touching short stories.

2. Some authors start writing as adults, but Isaac Bashevis Singer began writing at the age of fifteen.

3. I'm glad Singer wrote in English as well as Yiddish, for I can't read Yiddish.

4. C

5. Zlateh the goat is a farm animal, but she is also like a family pet.

6. Zlateh is old, and she doesn't produce much milk. *or* C

7. The father decides to sell the patient, good-natured old goat to buy Hannukah presents.

8. Zlateh is almost sold, but she proves that she is still valuable to the family.

9. Singer is a respected writer, and he won the Nobel Prize in literature in 1978.

10. You can buy a book of Singer's short stories, or I can lend you my copy.

◆ WORKSHEET 4: USING COMMAS C

Exercise: Proofreading

1. C

2. C

3. The island and its buildings, which were closed to the public for many years, are now part of the Statue of Liberty National Monument.

4. In 1990, Ellis Island, rebuilt as a museum, was officially opened to the public.

5. C

6. The museum's lobby, crowded with steamer trunks and other old baggage, is the visitors' first sight.

7. C

8. The Registry Room, which is on the second floor, sometimes held more than eleven thousand people.

9. The immigrants ‸ who came from many countries ‸ hoped to find freedom and a happier life in America.

10. *C*

◆ WORKSHEET 5: USING COMMAS D

Exercise: Proofreading

1. The whole class ‸ of course ‸ has read the novel *Old Yeller.*

2. Shana Alexander ‸ a former editor of *McCall's* ‸ was the main speaker.

3. Nathan ‸ do you own a thesaurus ‸ a dictionary of synonyms and antonyms?

4. The Galapagos Islands ‸ a group of volcanic islands in the Pacific Ocean ‸ were named for the Spanish word meaning "tortoise."

5. Rubber ‸ an elastic substance ‸ quickly restores itself to its original size and shape.

6. This bowl ‸ Mary Beth ‸ is made of clay found on Kilimanjaro ‸ the highest mountain in Africa.

7. For example ‸ the North Sea ‸ an arm of the Atlantic Ocean ‸ is rich in fish, natural gas, and oil.

8. Jamake Highwater ‸ a Blackfoot/Eastern Band Cherokee ‸ writes about the history of his people.

9. At Gettysburg ‸ a town in Pennsylvania ‸ an important battle of the Civil War was fought.

10. *C*

◆ WORKSHEET 6: USING COMMAS E

Exercise A: Proofreading

1. Although she did not win the nomination ‸ she raised many important issues.

2. On the desk in the den ‸ you will find your book.

3. Yes ‸ I enjoyed the fajitas that Ruben made.

4. Walking home from school ‸ Rosa saw a bird's nest in some bushes.

Exercise B: Proofreading

June 24 ‸ 1994

Dear Keno ‸

Well ‸ I'm glad you finally got to visit Durango ‸ Colorado. Going to my summer class ‸ I thought about your trip. Hey ‸ on your way back ‸ did you stop by your aunt's farm as you planned? When I heard you describe her horses ‸ I couldn't believe she has so many. I've moved, so write to me at 478 Maybird Street ‸ Athens ‸ Georgia.

Your friend ‸

Marta

◆ WORKSHEET 7: USING SEMICOLONS

Exercise: Proofreading

1. Tie these newspapers together with string ؛ put the aluminum cans in a bag.

2. I called Tom, Paul, and Francine ؛ and Fred called Amy, Carlos, and Brad.

3. Reading is my favorite pastime ؛ consequently ‸ I love to begin a new book.

4. We haven't seen the movie ؛ in fact ‸ we've never even heard of it.

5. Simone, Rita, and Hector use charcoal ؛ Anita uses paints.

◆ WORKSHEET 8: USING COLONS

Exercise A: Proofreading

1. The languages the exchange student speaks are as follows : English, German, French, and Spanish.

2. Our bus leaves at 6:23 A.M.

3. I learned three good watchwords for drivers : courtesy, caution, and judgment.

4. Please read Luke 3:7–8.

5. Dear Mayor Winston :

Exercise B: Proofreading

To All Employees :

You are invited to a luncheon at 1:30 P.M. on Friday. The speakers are as follows : Dr. Pérez, Mr. Feldman, and Ms. Puccini. Bring these supplies : your computer guide, a notebook, and two sharp pencils.

◆ WORKSHEET 9: REVIEW

Exercise A: Proofreading

1. Founded by Leonard and Bunny Brook ‸ the Sanctuary for Animals is a safe home for all kinds of animals ⊙

2. Through the years hundreds of stray ‸ unwanted ‸ and abused animals have found a home at the sanctuary ⊙

3. It is located on the Brooks' land in Westtown N⊙Y⊙

4. On their two hundred acres ‸ [optional comma] the Brooks take care of the following animals : camels ‸ lions ‸ elephants ‸ kangaroos ‸ dogs ‸ and cats ⊙

5. In addition ‸ Mr⊙ and Mrs⊙ Brook also raise chickens ‸ keep horses ‸ and look after their other farm animals ⊙

6. The Brooks ‸ their family ‸ and their friends care for the animals ؛ however ‸ they also let the animals work for themselves ⊙

7. Let me tell you how the animals work ⊙

8. The Brooks formed the Dawn Animal Agency ⌄ and their animals became actors and models ⊙

9. You may have seen their animals showing off in magazines ⌄ performing in movies or television shows ⌄ or helping to sell products in commercials ⊙

10. What an unusual ⌄ clever ⌄ caring way to help animals!

Exercise B: Proofreading

1. Toads and frogs ⌄ on the other hand ⌄ are amphibians ⊙

2. Some turtles live on land ⌄ others live in lakes ⌄ streams ⌄ or oceans ⊙

3. Although turtles have no teeth ⌄ they can bite with their strong ⌄ hard beaks ⊙

4. Yes ⌄ the terms *turtle* and *tortoise* are interchangeable ⌄ but *tortoise* usually refers to a land dweller ⊙

5. The African pancake tortoise ⌄ which has a flat ⌄ flexible shell ⌄ has a unique ability ⊙

6. Faced with a threat ⌄ it takes these measures ⌄ it crawls into a narrow crack in a rock ⌄ it takes a deep breath ⌄ and it wedges itself in tightly ⊙

7. Because some species of tortoises are endangered ⌄ they cannot be sold as pets ⊙

8. The following three species of tortoises live in the United States ⌄ the desert tortoise ⌄ the gopher tortoise ⌄ and the Texan tortoise ⊙

9. The gopher tortoise lives in the Southeast ⌄ the desert tortoise lives in the Southwest ⊙

10. The Indian star tortoise ⌄ considered an endangered species ⌄ is very rare ⌄ and I ⌄ as you can imagine ⌄ would like to see one ⊙

11. As this kind of tortoise grows older ⌄ its shell grows larger ⌄ the number of stars increases ⌄ and their pattern becomes more complex ⊙

12. The Indian star tortoise ⌄ an interesting animal ⌄ needs warmth ⌄ sun ⌄ and vegetables ⊙

13. Living in fresh water ⌄ soft-shelled turtles have long ⌄ flexible noses and fleshy lips ⊙

14. Their shells are not really soft ⌄ however ⌄ they are covered by smooth skin ⊙

15. Wanda ⌄ may I introduce you to my pet turtle ⌄ Pokey?

16. Pokey ⌄ who has been part of our family for years ⌄ is a red-eared turtle ⊙

17. When my parents got Pokey ⌄ he was only two inches in diameter

18. Pokey has been in my family for fifteen years ⌄ and he could easily live to be fifty ⊙

19. If you look at the design on Pokey's shell ⌄ you can get a good idea of his age ⊙

20. What a great pet Pokey is!

Exercise C: Proofreading

1. Yours truly ⌄

2. at the Diamond Co ⊙ at 10 ⌃ 30 A ⊙ M ⊙

3. Dear Uncle Ivan ⌄

4. Genesis 12 ⌃ 13

5. Dear Ms. Bridges ⌃

Exercise D: Proofreading

You're invited to a Splash Party on Thursday ⌄ May 26 ⌄ 1994.

Come to 224 Pine St ⊙ ⌄ Apartment 215, at 2 ⌃ 00 P ⌄ M ⊙ ⌃ call if you need a ride.

Bring the following items ⌄ bathing suit ⌄ clogs ⌄ towel ⌄ soap ⌄ and pool pass.

If you want to hear your favorite songs ⌄ bring some tapes ⌄ then we can dance.

Exercise E

(Answers will vary.)

1. My classes this year are as follows: geometry, biology, English, American history, and gym.

2. You will need these supplies for your project: paper, glue, and scissors.

3. So far we have studied the following punctuation marks: period, comma, semicolon, and colon.

4. Meet me at the mall at 3:00 P.M.

5. My favorite foods are pasta, spinach, and granola.

Chapter 14: Punctuation

◆ WORKSHEET 1: UNDERLINING (ITALICS)

Exercise: Proofreading

1. humor, u, o
2. triathlon
3. Newsweek
4. Norwalk Valley News
5. La Bamba
6. Oceanic
7. Dances with Wolves
8. The Time of Your Life
9. Spirit of St. Louis, Flyer, Gemini IV
10. The Summer of the Swans

◆ WORKSHEET 2: DIRECT AND INDIRECT QUOTATIONS

Exercise: Proofreading

1. C

2. At the same time, Bob whispered, "It's only a movie—calm down!"

3. C

4. I quietly replied, "I'm sorry."

5. "You shouldn't have screamed," he complained.

6. "From now on I promise I'll try to be quiet," I said.

7. When the lights came on, Bob said, "It's time to go."

8. C

9. "I can't help yelling when I'm scared," I explained.

10. "Yes, but you were afraid even during the credits," Bob protested.

◆ WORKSHEET 3: SETTING OFF DIRECT QUOTATIONS

Exercise: Proofreading

1. "Oh, like the clothes Mr. Johnson showed us in class!" Janell exclaimed.

2. Elton asked, "Have you read any Ashley Bryan books about African culture?"

3. Janell replied, "I've read *Beat the Story-Drum, Pum-Pum*."

4. "I really liked that one," Elton said. "I really enjoy African folk tales."

5. "I think *Walk Together Children* is excellent," Janell said.

6. "Is that one," Elton asked, "about spirituals?"

7. "That's right," Janell answered. "Ashley Bryan believes that spirituals are the United States' greatest contribution to world music."

8. She added, "He grew up in New York City and began writing stories and drawing when he was still in kindergarten."

9. "Did you know," Elton asked, "that he illustrated his own books?"

10. "Bryan made woodcuts to illustrate *Walk Together Children*," he added.

◆ WORKSHEET 4: PUNCTUATING DIALOGUE

Exercise: Revising

Our drama teacher is strict about play rehearsals. Did you hear her say, "Do not miss class or rehearsals if you want to be in the play"?

"What will happen if we miss a rehearsal?" Sonia asked.

"You will be replaced, whatever your part is," Ms. Sibilia answered. "There are more students who want to be in the play than there are parts available. If you miss rehearsal, someone will be more than glad to take your place. Does everyone understand this?"

"Yes, and I'm one of the someones," replied Cordelia. "I think I'll learn everyone's lines just in case I'm called on to take over!"

◆ WORKSHEET 5: OTHER USES OF QUOTATION MARKS

Exercise: Proofreading

1. Lani yelled to me, "Tracey, Mom says, 'Get in here right now!'"

2. The most interesting chapter in *The Sea Around Us* is "The Birth of an Island."

3. "Didn't Benjamin Franklin once say, 'Time is money'?" asked Myra.

4. "My favorite Langston Hughes poem is 'As I Grew Older,'" said Mona.

5. *Nova*'s program tonight is "Man on the Moon."

6. The latest issue of *Seascience* has an article entitled "The Things Sharks Swallow."

7. "Do you know which character asked, 'What's in a name?' in *Romeo and Juliet*?" I asked.

8. "Yes," answered Sylvia. "My mother used to say that to me when I was a little girl. She also read the poem 'Who Is Sylvia.'"

9. "If you like videos," said Van, "you should read the 'Video Talk' article in *Electro World*."

10. There is an article called "The Customers Always Write" in today's newspaper.

◆ WORKSHEET 6: REVIEW

Exercise A: Proofreading

1. IQ

2. DQ—"How can we dance if the sea gets rough?" asked Mrs. Colby.

3. DQ—"My dear," her husband replied, "we'll just rock with the waves."

4. DQ—"What's that out there?" Clive asked.

5. DQ—Mrs. Colby asked, "Did you hear the steward shout, 'It looks like an iceberg!'?"

Exercise B: Revising

"Are you going to watch the programs on Classic Theater this fall?" asked Thom. "The Miami Herald had an article about what will be on, and the writer said, 'Don't miss an episode.'"

"Time also recommended them," said Ginny, "but I can't watch the one tonight. I have to finish my book report on To Kill a Mockingbird. I wish I could remember whether Scout's father's name has one t or two. And which adjective do you think describes the book better, suspenseful or exciting?"

"How about intense," said Thom. "By the way, have you read the poem 'Stopping by Woods on a Snowy Evening'? It's one of my favorites."

"Mine too," said Ginny. "Thanks for calling, but I must get my book report finished, and it's nearly time for you to watch the first episode of Clouds over Alaska."

Chapter 15: Punctuation

◆ WORKSHEET 1: USING APOSTROPHES TO SHOW POSSESSION

Exercise

1. the party's nominee
2. the babies' clothes
3. my sister's grades
4. the guests' name tags
5. Odysseus' journey
6. the goose's corn
7. anyone's footprints
8. everybody's opinions
9. their books
10. the women's clothing

◆ WORKSHEET 2: USING APOSTROPHES IN CONTRACTIONS

Exercise

1. We'd
2. car's; hasn't
3. wasn't
4. Who's
5. won't; you've
6. I'm; you'll
7. We'll; won't
8. Ann's; hasn't
9. It's; isn't
10. I'm; they'll; it's

◆ WORKSHEET 3: USING CONTRACTIONS AND POSSESSIVE PRONOUNS

Exercise A

1. CON; They're
2. PP
3. PP
4. CON; it's
5. CON; There's
6. CON; he's
7. PP
8. CON; they're
9. PP
10. CON; Who's

Exercise B

1. Haven't
2. their
3. Whose
4. couldn't
5. weren't

◆ WORKSHEET 4: USING APOSTROPHES IN PLURALS

Exercise A

1. *yes*'s; *no*'s
2. *i*'s
3. *2*'s
4. *4*'s; *9*'s
5. *and*'s
6. *m*'s; *n*'s
7. *5*'s
8. *r*'s
9. *X*'s; *O*'s
10. *why*'s; *wherefore*'s

Exercise B: Proofreading

Dear Yoshi,

I'm writing to tell you why 7's are lucky! You'll never believe it! I won a contest by guessing how many beans were in a jar! My winning guess was 777. What's the prize? I won seven movie tickets. Let me know if you'd like to use one.

Do you think they used all 7's in the number on purpose? It's funny if they did because the address of the theater has three 5's in it and no 7's, and the name of the theater is Super 8's! So 7's were just a lucky guess.

Your pal,

Emily

◆ WORKSHEET 5: USING HYPHENS

Exercise: Proofreading

1. I read twenty-two books last summer.

2. One of my favorites was a book by Virginia Hamilton called *Paul Robeson,* a biog-raphy.

3. Paul Robeson was an African American singer and actor. He played the title role in the play *The Emperor Jones.*

4. Because of the political situation in the United States, he lived in Eng-land for several years.

5. If I could be one-tenth the singer Paul Robeson was, I would be happy.

◆ WORKSHEET 6: USING PARENTHESES AND DASHES

Exercise A: Proofreading

1. (my favorite sport)
2. (1843–1929)
3. (My old one stopped working.)
4. (shär' lə mān')
5. (she's a friend of mine)

Exercise B: Proofreading

1. —I can't remember where I read this—
2. —can't you guess?—
3. —I really want to see his concert—
4. —here they come now—
5. —that is, after you've learned the strokes—

◆ WORKSHEET 7: REVIEW

Exercise A

Singular Possessive	Plural Possessive
1. star's	stars'
2. lady's	ladies'
3. monkey's	monkeys'
4. mouse's	mice's
5. roof's	roofs'
6. tomato's	tomatoes'
7. family's	families'
8. tooth's	teeth's
9. dish's	dishes'
10. leaf's	leaves'

Exercise B

1. our *or* ours
2. somebody's
3. your *or* yours
4. its
5. whose

Exercise C

1. couldn't
2. here's
3. who's
4. they're
5. what's
6. aren't
7. it's
8. wasn't
9. I'm
10. we're

Exercise D

1. it's	3. its	5. You're
2. Whose	4. Their	

Exercise E: Proofreading

1. Here's the magazine article about the scientists digging up the dinosaur bones in Wyoming in the 1980's.

2. Someone's bicycle has been out on our porch for a week, and I don't know whose it is.

3. Mrs. Acuna hasn't decided yet whether to get the CD player for her brother-in-law's birthday; he'll be twenty-three.

4. If you put lines through your 7's, as they do in Europe, sometimes they look like F's.

5. I'd rather use my nickname than my real name because I like to write y's.

Exercise F: Proofreading

(Answers may vary.)

1. The best gift you can give Mom and Dad̄—they'll love it̄—is a weekend free from chores.

2. Our school's engineer (Anne's uncle) won an award for bravery.

3. Help me move this tablē—I know it's heavȳ—so we can put the bookcase by the wall.

4. Sojourner Truth (1797–1883) and Harriet Tubman (1820–1913) were famous abolitionists.

5. I have always dreamed of owninḡ—believe it or not̄—a bright purple motorcycle.

Chapter 16: Spelling and Vocabulary

◆ WORKSHEET 1: IMPROVING YOUR SPELLING

Exercise A: Proofreading

1. documentary	3. expert	5. laboratory
2. different	4. probably	

Exercise B

1. a-tro-cious	3. hab-i-tat	5. sci-en-tist
2. fright-ened	4. re-search	

◆ WORKSHEET 2: ROOTS

Exercise A

(Definitions may vary.)

1. transportation—a means of taking people or cargo from one place to another

2. contradict—to say something against or to disagree with

3. interject—to insert a remark in a conversation; to throw in a comment or question

4. revise—to look at carefully in order to rework or correct

5. depend—to be determined by something else

Exercise B

(Answers will vary.)

1. Better methods of transportation opened up new markets in the West.

2. Didn't the speaker contradict himself three times?

3. Feel free to interject comments at any time during the discussion.

4. Revise the sentences, correcting errors in pronoun usage.

5. Our success will depend upon our cooperation.

◆ WORKSHEET 3: PREFIXES

Exercise

(Definitions may vary.)

1. disjoined—separated
2. misguided—wrongly guided; led astray
3. uneasy—not easy; uncomfortable
4. transatlantic—across the Atlantic
5. prewriting—before writing
6. incurable—not able to be cured or healed
7. refilled—filled again
8. extraordinary—beyond the ordinary
9. foremost—first in rank or place
10. substandard—below an established standard

◆ WORKSHEET 4: SUFFIXES

Exercise

(Definitions may vary.)

1. justifiable—able to be justified or defended
2. resentful—full of resentment; jealous and bitter
3. moisten—to make moist or wet
4. measurement—the result of measuring (the size or amount)
5. ideally—in the way characteristic of an ideal; in a perfect or most desired way
6. realize—to make appear real
7. editor—one who edits
8. picturesque—in the style of a picture; scenic or quaint
9. thrifty—condition of showing thrift or being economical
10. hardship—a hard condition; a difficulty

◆ WORKSHEET 5: SPELLING RULES A

Exercise A

1. friend	5. neither	9. brief
2. neighbor	6. chief	10. foreign
3. nieces	7. leisurely	
4. believe	8. relieved	

Exercise B: Proofreading

(The first item in each pair is the incorrect spelling. The second item is the correct spelling.)

1. prosede—proceed
2. excedes—exceeds

3. C

4. superceded—superseded

5. receed—recede

◆ WORKSHEET 6: SPELLING RULES B

Exercise A

1. illegible
2. unnecessary
3. impartial
4. inoffensive
5. immortal
6. misspell
7. dissatisfy
8. disapprove
9. misunderstand
10. overrule

Exercise B

1. hopefully
2. happiness
3. advancement
4. desirable
5. truly
6. easily
7. dropped
8. baying
9. hurried
10. advantageous

◆ WORKSHEET 7: PLURALS OF NOUNS A

Exercise A

1. wishes
2. pianos
3. puppies
4. beliefs
5. selves

Exercise B: Proofreading

[1] Of the ~~essaies~~ *essays* I've read, "When I Was a Boy on the Ranch" is my favorite. [2] Dobie writes about life on ~~ranchs~~ *ranches* in southwestern Texas. [3] Dobie recalls that the young ranch hands liked to copy the ~~activitys~~ *activities* of the cowpunchers they admired. [4] The Western ~~heros~~ *heroes* were usually building fences and tending the livestock.

[5] Dobie says that he had several horses to ride by the time he was eight ~~yeares~~ *years* old.

◆ WORKSHEET 8: PLURALS OF NOUNS B

Exercise A

1. *m*'s
2. scissors
3. 1930's
4. children
5. Chinese
6. mothers-in-law
7. governors-elect
8. *if*'s
9. two-year-olds
10. side-wheelers

Exercise B

(Sentences will vary.)

1. Both amusement parks have old merry-go-rounds.

2. It's important to think about all the *if*'s before making a decision.

3. Are those *?*'s or 7's?

4. While many moose may live in a given area, they do not form herds.

5. I have five sisters and five brothers-in-law.

◆ WORKSHEET 9: SPELLING NUMBERS

Exercise A: Proofreading

1. 730
2. third
3. one thousand
4. Five
5. 800

Exercise B

Paragraphs will vary. Students should follow rules for spelling numbers at the beginnings of and within sentences.

◆ WORKSHEET 10: USING CONTEXT CLUES A

Exercise

1. j	3. i	5. h	7. b	9. f
2. g	4. a	6. d	8. e	10. c

◆ WORKSHEET 11: USING CONTEXT CLUES B

Exercise

(Answers may vary.)

1. not anxious or distressed; relaxed
2. put off or delayed
3. a type of sea bird, like a gull
4. angry
5. miscellaneous pieces
6. pronounce clearly
7. cooking
8. one-colored
9. city
10. dry

◆ WORKSHEET 12: CHOOSING THE RIGHT WORD

Exercise A

1. S, b—broke
2. A, a—quiet
3. A, e—calm
4. S, c—well-known
5. S, d—steps

Exercise B

(Answers will vary.)

1. The aroma of fresh bread awoke us.

2. We searched for the source of the odor and finally found a dead rat in the cellar.

Exercise C

(Answers may vary.)

1. illumination; come to rest

2. guide; made of lead, a type of metal

◆ WORKSHEET 13: REVIEW

Exercise A

1. bu-reau
2. em-bar-rass
3. dis-ci-pline
4. im-me-di-ate-ly
5. gen-u-ine

Exercise B

(Answers will vary.)

1. respect, speculate
2. reduce, education
3. transport, portable
4. vocal, vocation
5. television, visionary

Exercise C

(Definitions may vary.)

1. antisocial—against, opposing; opposed to society

2. jealous—characterized by; characterized by discontent or resentment because of another's influence

3. misfire—badly, not, wrongly; to fail to ignite

4. kingdom—state, condition; domain

5. gritty—condition, quality; of, like, or containing rough particles of sand or stone

Exercise D

1. leisure	3. neighbor	5. yield
2. friend	4. proceed	

Exercise E

1. dislocate	5. business	9. payment
2. mainly	6. noticeable	10. merriment
3. arguing	7. trapped	
4. unnatural	8. barely	

Exercise F

1. (Ages may vary, but should be spelled out.)

2. mixes

3. men

4. (Answers will vary. Ordinal numbers should be spelled out.)

5. mothers-in-law

6. igloos

7. fifty-two

8. donkeys

9. Sioux

10. (Answers may vary.) gloomy

11. potatoes

12. countries

13. (Answers may vary.) alone

14. A's

15. giraffes

Exercise G

1. f	2. c	3. b	4. a	5. e

Chapter 17: The Writing Process

◆ WORKSHEET 1: FREEWRITING

Exercise A

(Answers will vary.)

Water. Rivers, lakes, oceans. Covers most of earth's surface. Needed for life. Water to drink, water to bathe and wash clothes. Don't take water for granted, some people don't have enough water. Need to protect our water from pollution—no dumping of factory chemicals in rivers and lakes. Waterfalls in mountains, beautiful, source of electrical power, loud.

Exercise B

(Answers will vary.)

Waterfalls. Niagara Falls great for people on honeymoon. Some waterfalls not so big, but still pretty. Whitewater rafting, going over waterfall, how would that feel? Exciting, scary, loud, wet, makes me dizzy to think of it. Jungle waterfalls in Africa, South America, what animals and fish could you see there?

◆ WORKSHEET 2: BRAINSTORMING

Exercise A

(Answers will vary.)

Subject you chose: space aliens

Brainstorming notes:

intelligent life on other planets	life forms adapted to own planet
What would they look like?	how to survive in other atmospheres
UFO's—alien spaceships or what?	how to make friends with them
communication	travel—faster spaceships needed
Find out how they handle pollution.	
old movies, aliens as enemy	new languages to learn
travel to other planets, galaxies	new clothes, music, dances
colonies of aliens on earth	exotic foods from other planets
colonies of humans on other planets	

Exercise B

(Answers will vary.)

Idea you chose: UFO's—alien spaceships or what?

Explanation: Many people report seeing UFO's, unidentified flying objects. Sometimes U.S. government says they're weather balloons. But I've seen odd photos of things in the air that look like spaceships. I wonder if they are. After all, what makes us think we're the only creatures in the universe that can build a spaceship? There are so many galaxies out there—maybe there is intelligent life on other planets.

◆ WORKSHEET 3: CLUSTERING AND QUESTIONING

Exercise A

(Answers will vary.)

Exercise B

(Answers will vary.)

Subject: Atlanta to host Olympics

Who will be representing the United States?

What new events will be added?

When will the games begin?

Where in the Atlanta area will the games be held?

Why was Atlanta chosen?

How do athletes qualify for the Olympics?

◆ WORKSHEET 4: READING, LISTENING, IMAGINING

Exercise A

Answers will vary. You may want students to list the sources of their information.

Exercise B

Answers will vary. Students' notes should demonstrate careful listening and questioning.

Exercise C

Responses will vary. Remember that recent book and movie plots have shown that "What if?" questions can include fantasy and science fiction. Encourage students to make their plot outlines brief.

◆ WORKSHEET 5: PURPOSE AND AUDIENCE

Exercise A

(Answers may vary.)

1. to be creative
2. to explain or inform
3. to persuade
4. to express your feelings
5. to explain or inform

Exercise B

Have students explain how they arrive at their decisions. Sentences 1 and 2 belong in the report. Sentence 3 is unrelated to the topic and is a personal comment. Sentence 4 is about an Italian, not a Hawaiian, volcano. Sentence 5 supplies knowledge that classmates probably already have, and the sentence does not apply specifically to Hawaiian volcanoes.

◆ WORKSHEET 6: ARRANGING IDEAS

Exercise A

3, 5, 1, 4, 2

Exercise B

1. I
2. S *or* L
3. L
4. I
5. L

◆ WORKSHEET 7: USING VISUALS A

Exercise A

(Charts may vary.)

	United States	China
Area (sq. mi.)	3,600,000	3,690,000
Population	more than 250,000,000	more than 1,100,000,000
Government	republic	Communist regime

Exercise B

Information in diagrams will vary, but each diagram should have information that shows how the two kinds of music are similar in the overlapping portion of the circles and information that shows how the two kinds of music are different in the outside parts of the circles.

◆ WORKSHEET 8: USING VISUALS B

Exercise A

Information in diagrams will vary, but each should be in tree form.

Exercise B

Information in diagrams will vary, but each diagram should show events or steps in chronological order.

◆ WORKSHEET 9: WRITING A FIRST DRAFT

Exercise A

Answers will vary. Students should write freely with no concern for grammar, usage, or mechanics.

Exercise B

Answers will vary. Ideas should be organized in coherent order.

◆ WORKSHEET 10: SELF-EVALUATION

Exercise

(Evaluations will vary. You may wish to require a minimum of four statements.)

1. The writing is interesting and informative.
2. The organization needs work.
3. The voice in the next to the last sentence is inappropriate to the purpose and audience.
4. The first sentence has too much information for a lead.

◆ WORKSHEET 11: PEER EVALUATION

Exercise

(Answers will vary.)

1. Could the first sentence be rewritten to better grab the reader's attention?
2. What is the main idea of the paragraph?
3. If the main idea concerns the Chinese language, should the discussion about the importance of English be moved to another paragraph?
4. Should all statements about the three languages discussed be in order of importance—for example, all statements about Chinese first, then the ones about English, then those about Spanish?
5. Does the discussion about Japanese kanji distract the reader from the discussion of the Chinese language?

◆ WORKSHEET 12: REVISING

Exercise

(Answers may vary.)

1. These two sentences express the main idea of the paragraph.
2. *Shrine* is a more specific word.
3. The sentence emphasizes the importance of the Curies' gift.
4. The words *refused to* show that not taking out a patent was a deliberate act, not just an oversight.
5. The cut sentence expresses an opinion, which has no place in an informative paragraph.

26   CHAPTER 18

◆ WORKSHEET 13: PROOFREADING AND PUBLISHING

Exercise A: Proofreading

Communication is faster today than it was just a few hundred years ago. Queen Isabella did not get word of Columbus's discovery in 1942 [1492] until five months, after. After Columbus had landed. France did not get word that Lincoln had been assassinated until two weeks after his death. in [In] 1969, [optional comma] Neil Armstrong's message from the moon took 1.3 seconds to arrive on earth. In the 1990's, [optional comma] we have fiber-optic wires that can conduct 800 million pieces of information in one second. It's no wonder that some people think we may be able to get information about events *before* they occur!

Exercise B

(Answers will vary.)

1. I might write a letter to the editor of a science magazine.

2. I could read the work aloud to a science class.

3. I could share the piece with friends.

Chapter 18: Paragraph and Composition Structure

◆ WORKSHEET 1: THE PARAGRAPH'S MAIN IDEA

Exercise

(Answers may vary.)

1. writing instruments over time
2. the first lamps
3. what a stethoscope is used for
4. where silicon comes from
5. different art media

◆ WORKSHEET 2: THE TOPIC SENTENCE

Exercise

1. Storytellers were an important part of the Iroquois way of life.

2. In those days, Iroquois women dressed both for warmth and protection as well as for the sake of beauty.

3. The jobs of the Iroquois were divided between men and women.

4. The Iroquois played what has become our modern-day game of lacrosse.

5. Canoes were the basic means of Iroquois transport.

◆ WORKSHEET 3: USING SENSORY DETAILS

Exercise A

(Answers may vary.)

Sight: 100-foot slide, aqua water

Hearing: whooping, splashing

Touch: tubes floating gently, hot sun, sore body

Taste: fish, mouthfuls of water

Smell: chlorine, sunblock

Exercise B

(Answers will vary.)

Topic: the best surprise ever

	Detail 1	Detail 2
Sight	balloons	presents
Hearing	birthday song	shouts of "Surprise!"
Touch	hugs from friends	my new baseball glove
Taste	popcorn	fruit punch
Smell	leather of new glove	chocolate cake

◆ WORKSHEET 4: USING FACTS AND EXAMPLES

Exercise A

Cross out these facts:

In many supermarkets today, customers are asked whether they want paper or plastic bags.

Today, people are developing new ways to recycle plastics.

Exercise B

(Answers will vary.)

1. Examples—First we had a thunderstorm, and then we had a stickball game.

2. Facts—The first Olympic games were held in ancient Greece. The modern Olympic games began in Greece in 1896.

◆ WORKSHEET 5: UNITY IN PARAGRAPHS

Exercise

1. The apparent face of the moon is really just craters.
2. Wheat was scarce.
3. She wondered if the Cardinals game would be on television that evening.
4. You can also find canoes that are made to carry either one or two people.

◆ WORKSHEET 6: COHERENCE IN PARAGRAPHS A

Exercise

1. first, when, to, Before, to, there
2. First, Then, after, there, from, above
3. After, to, immediately, to, Next, in, In, along, until
4. When, from, down, Finally, to, where
5. following, to, around, There, into

◆ WORKSHEET 7: COHERENCE IN PARAGRAPHS B

Exercise

(Answers may vary.)

1. but   3. and   5. since
2. As a result   4. because   6. Another

HRW material copyrighted under notice appearing earlier in this work.

7. To begin with   9. although

8. therefore   10. however

◆ WORKSHEET 8:   DESCRIPTION: USING SPATIAL ORDER

Exercise A

giant float

entrance to moving sidewalk

World of Tomorrow Pavilion

Future Rides

Future Food and Beverage Center

Future World Gift Shop

first-aid station

Exercise B

(Answers will vary.)

Near the entrance to the park is a moving sidewalk. If you don't find it easily, look for the giant float of cartoon characters who point to it. Take the sidewalk to the third and last stop. There you will see the Future Food and Beverage Center. Just behind it is the Future World Gift Shop.

◆ WORKSHEET 9:   NARRATION: USING CHRONOLOGICAL ORDER

Exercise

(Answers will vary.)

1. Each list should contain three or more events pertaining to the chosen topic and arranged in chronological order.

2. Each list should contain three or more steps involving performing the chosen activity and arranged in chronological order.

3. Each explanation should relate a sequence of events in chronological order, showing the cause-and-effect relationships among events.

◆ WORKSHEET 10:   CLASSIFICATION: USING LOGICAL ORDER

Exercise A

Answers will vary, but each topic should have at least one valid comparison statement and one valid contrast statement.

Exercise B

Answers will vary. All sentences should be about Clydesdales, and each paragraph should move from a general definition to more specific details about this particular breed.

◆ WORKSHEET 11:   EVALUATION: USING ORDER OF IMPORTANCE

Exercise

Answers will vary. Each response should follow the example's structure, state an opinion, and offer three reasons supporting that opinion.

◆ WORKSHEET 12:   PLANNING A COMPOSITION

Exercise A

(Answers will vary.)

Recycling can save resources.

Exercise B

(Answers will vary.)

1. Early pioneer women often worked as builders and farmers in the American West.

2. Many people in the United States decorate their cars in unusual and elaborate ways.

◆ WORKSHEET 13:   EARLY PLANS

Exercise A

(Answers may vary.)

1. Yard care	2. Exercise	3. Hobbies
mowing the lawn	aerobics	stamp collecting
weeding the garden	running	model ship building
trimming hedges	swimming	painting

Exercise B

1, 5, 2, 4, 3

◆ WORKSHEET 14:   FORMAL OUTLINES

Exercise

II. B. Marrow inside bones

III. A. Heart that pumps blood

IV. C. Lungs that hold oxygen for the body

V. B. Spinal cord that is the "roadway" for nerves

VI. B. Involuntary muscle

◆ WORKSHEET 15:   THE INTRODUCTION

Exercise

1. stating an intriguing or startling fact

2. asking a question

3. telling an anecdote

4. stating an intriguing or startling fact

5. telling an anecdote

◆ WORKSHEET 16:   THE BODY

Exercise

(Answers will vary.)

1. **Main idea of composition:** Various animals hibernate throughout the winter.

2. **Supporting idea 2:** People should eat lots of fruits, whole grains, and vegetables.

3. **Main idea of composition:** Gift-giving has different purposes in different societies.

4. **Main idea of composition:** Dinosaurs varied greatly in size.

5. **Supporting idea 2:** Human babies don't learn to walk until they are about one year old.

◆ **WORKSHEET 17:   UNITY AND COHERENCE IN COMPOSITIONS**

Exercise A
1. Rabbits have strong hind legs, also.
2. Sharks do not develop cancer.

Exercise B
(Answers may vary.)
1. First   2. Therefore

◆ **WORKSHEET 18:   THE CONCLUSION**

Exercise
(Answers may vary.)
1. Horses are truly magnificent animals.
2. Clothing that is outdated today may be the newest fashion in the future.

Chapter 19: The Research Report

◆ **WORKSHEET 1: CHOOSING A SUBJECT**

Exercise A
Answers will vary. Have students continue writing on separate sheets of paper if necessary.

Exercise B
Answers will vary. You may want to allow students to work on this exercise outside of school.

◆ **WORKSHEET 2: NARROWING A SUBJECT**

Exercise
(Answers will vary.)
Subject: pets

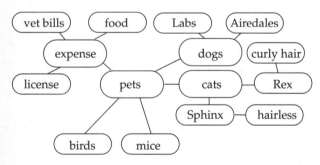

Topic: unusual breeds of domestic cats

◆ **WORKSHEET 3: THINKING ABOUT AUDIENCE AND PURPOSE**

Exercise A
Answers will vary. Suggest to students that they pick topics they are already familiar with.

Exercise B
A good report would use sentences 2 and 4. The audience already knows the material in sentences 1 and 5. Sentence 3 is a personal opinion and does not belong in a research report.

◆ **WORKSHEET 4: MAKING AN EARLY PLAN AND ASKING QUESTIONS**

Exercise
(Answers will vary.)
Topic: schools in Japan
Question 1: Who controls schools in Japan?
Question 2: What are the major courses taught?
Question 3: When do students go to school?
Question 4: Where are the schools located?
Question 5: Why do Japanese students excel?
Question 6: How are the school days divided?

◆ **WORKSHEET 5: FINDING AND EVALUATING SOURCES**

Exercise
(Answers will vary.)
Print Sources: books, magazines, encyclopedias
Nonprint Sources: videotapes, slides, interviews with people who have special knowledge about the topic

◆ **WORKSHEET 6: LISTING SOURCES AND TAKING NOTES**

Exercise A
(Author names will vary.)

> 1
>
> Appleton, Karima. Surviving Middle School.
>   New York: Ican, 1993.

Exercise B
(Answers will vary.)

Brooks describes city life of young African Americans. "Home" from *Maud Martha*—family may lose home because can't pay mortgage. Not autobiography, "but the Home Owners' Loan Corporation that intrudes in 'Home' *was* a reality for the young author." Brooks later won Pulitzer Prize.

◆ **WORKSHEET 7: ORGANIZING AND OUTLINING INFORMATION**

Exercise
(Answers may vary.)
 I. Floods
    A. Coastal floods
    B. Inland floods
       1. Mississippi River
       2. Missouri River
 II. Tornadoes
    A. Why tornadoes occur
    B. Where tornadoes occur
       1. Tornado Alley
       2. Tornadoes outside the "Alley"

◆ **WORKSHEET 8: WRITING A FIRST DRAFT**

Exercise

(Answers will vary.)

   Killer bees can live where the winters are mild. They will be year-round residents as far north as San Francisco and southern Maryland. They will also live all year in southern Texas and in Arizona, Alabama, Mississippi, Louisiana, Virginia, North Carolina, and South Carolina (1, pp. 34–35). In the summer, killer bees will live in the northern states. They will die there when it gets cold (2, p. 72).

◆ **WORKSHEET 9: EVALUATING AND REVISING**

Exercise

(Answers may vary.)

   1. The information was out of place. It logically follows the fact that bees "come after people in a big swarm."

   2. The information is necessary to contrast Africanized bees with native bees.

   3. The sentence states the writer's opinion rather than a fact or an expert's ideas. It makes the paragraph sound too informal.

4. The quotation marks show words that are a direct quotation from a source.

◆ **WORKSHEET 10: PROOFREADING AND PUBLISHING**

Exercise A: Proofreading

   Spirituals were ~~sang~~ *sung* by slaves on ~~southern~~ *Southern* plantations. Frederick ~~douglass~~ *Douglass* a former slave, said that slaves were generally expected to sing as well as to work. Most of the songs were very ~~sorowful~~ *sorrowful*. Many of ~~them~~ *those* spirituals are still sung today. They were often about a better life to come.

   Some of the spirituals had codes in them. For example, "Go Down, Moses" is a spiritual based on the ~~bible~~ *Bible* story about the Israelites, who were slaves in ~~egypt~~ *Egypt*. Moses was sent to ask the pharoah to set the Israelites free⊙ To the African American slaves singing this ~~Spiritual~~ *spiritual*, the words were also a plea to their masters to "Let my people go."

Exercise B

(Answers will vary.)

   1. publish in school newspaper

   2. display on bulletin board

   3. read aloud to class

   4. send to local church publication

   5. illustrate and put in a binder, and then give to school library as a resource

Resources

◆ **WORKSHEET 1: THE DEWEY DECIMAL SYSTEM**

Exercise A

1. The Arts	6. Philosophy
2. Languages	7. History
3. Technology	8. Literature
4. Religion	9. Science
5. Social Sciences	10. General Works

Exercise B

1. F   2. N   3. N   4. F   5. F

◆ **WORKSHEET 2: THE CARD CATALOG**

Exercise

1. T	3. A	5. T	7. S	9. T
2. S	4. S	6. A	8. A	10. A

◆ **WORKSHEET 3: THE PARTS OF A BOOK**

Exercise

1. copyright page	6. bibliography
2. glossary	7. index
3. index	8. table of contents
4. copyright page	9. title page
5. table of contents	10. appendix

◆ **WORKSHEET 4: USING REFERENCE MATERIALS**

Exercise

(Answers may vary.)

1. biographical reference
2. *Readers' Guide to Periodical Literature*
3. book of synonyms
4. atlas
5. encyclopedia
6. almanac
7. microform
8. vertical file
9. reference book about literature *or* encyclopedia
10. special biographical reference *or* encyclopedia

◆ **WORKSHEET 5: USING THE NEWSPAPER**

Exercise

Answers will vary. Check your newspaper to verify students' statements.

◆ **WORKSHEET 6: USING THE DICTIONARY A**

Exercise

(Answers will vary for nos. 3 and 4.)

1. Polish
2. Japan and China

3. In Australia, the term means a temporary return to a native way of life. In Great Britain, it means a walking tour.

4. In such a case, the general would mean that it was an overwhelming or one-sided victory.

5. Valhalla

◆ WORKSHEET 7: USING THE DICTIONARY B

Exercise A

1. no	3. first	5. dīme *or* dim
2. du-pli-cate	4. second	

Exercise B

1. adjective	5. preposition	9. adverb
2. adverb	6. conjunction	10. interjection
3. verb	7. pronoun	
4. noun	8. adjective	

Exercise C

(Answers for no. 5 may vary.)

1. sons-in-law

2. swam

3. It is plural. (The singular form is *louse*.)

4. amoebas *or* amoebae

5. normalcy, normality, normally

◆ WORKSHEET 8: USING THE DICTIONARY C

Exercise A

(Answers will vary depending on the dictionaries used.)

1. Ger	5. Yidd	9. Eng
2. OFr	6. Chin	10. Iran
3. Sp	7. OE	
4. Ar	8. Dan	

Exercise B

(Answers may vary slightly for nos. 1 and 4.)

1. *Boycott* comes from the name of Captain C. C. Boycott, an Irish land agent.

2. *Australis* means "southern."

3. *Radar* is a combination of the words *radio detecting and ranging*.

4. *Corps* comes from the Old French *corps, cors,* meaning "body"; it originally came from the Latin *corpus,* also meaning "body."

5. The letters *AWOL* stand for "absent without leave."

◆ WORKSHEET 9: USING THE DICTIONARY D

Exercise A

(Answers may vary depending on the dictionaries used.)

1. To a printer, *composition* means "the setting up of type for printing."

2. In card playing, *draw* means "to take or get (cards)" or "to cause (cards) to be played."

3. In golf, *draw* means "to cause a ball to curve from a straight course."

4. In music, *first* means "being highest in pitch or carrying the leading part."

Exercise B

(Answers may vary.)

1. heroically

2. in mint condition; a mint of ideas

3. something ready for use; available money or property; something that a country can use to its advantage; means of accomplishing something; source of strength; ability to deal promptly and effectively with problems

4. clumsy; awkward; inept

◆ WORKSHEET 10: PERSONAL LETTERS

Exercise A

Letters will vary. Advise students they may write to a real or imaginary friend.

Exercise B

Letters will vary. Students may write to a real or imaginary relative.

◆ WORKSHEET 11: SOCIAL LETTERS

Exercises A

1. R	2. T	3. I	4. T	5. I

Exercise B

Letters will vary but should express regret politely.

◆ WORKSHEET 12: THE PARTS OF A BUSINESS LETTER

Exercise

1. S	2. B	3. I	4. H	5. C

◆ WORKSHEET 13: TYPES OF BUSINESS LETTERS

Exercise

Letters will vary. Students who choose option 2 or 3 may want to actually send their letters.

◆ WORKSHEET 14: ADDRESSING ENVELOPES AND COMPLETING PRINTED FORMS

Exercise A

Envelopes will vary. Point out to students that most addresses take only three lines.

Exercise B

1. I	2. C	3. I	4. C	5. C

◆ WORKSHEET 15: MANUSCRIPT STYLE A

Exercise

1. I	3. I	5. I	7. I	9. I
2. C	4. I	6. C	8. C	10. I

◆ WORKSHEET 16: MANUSCRIPT STYLE B

Exercise: Proofreading

1. My teacher, M.L.K. Johnson, is an admirer of author Pearl S. Buck (1892–1973).

2. Pearl S. Buck was born in West Virginia, but spent most of her life in China.

3. Mr. Johnson says that as a child, Buck spoke Chinese before she learned English.

4. At 2:00 P.M. on the Public Broadcasting Service, we are going to see PBS's dramatization of *The Big Wave,* a story that Ms. Buck wrote about Japan.

5. A professor spoke about Buck's writing and told us she won the Nobel Prize for literature in 1938.

◆ WORKSHEET 17: MANUSCRIPT STYLE C

Exercise: Proofreading

1. On July 8, the nomination was not decided until the fifty-seventh ballot.

2. The first chairperson [*or* chair] of the committee was Laura McGown.

3. There are seventeen wild turkeys resting in that field.

4. Everyone coming to the picnic should bring a plate, a cup, and tableware. *or* People coming to the picnic should bring their own plates, cups, and tableware.

5. It took us thirteen days to find twenty-five pictures for the collage.

◆ WORKSHEET 18: REVIEW

Exercise A

1. subject   3. title   5. subject
2. subject   4. author

Exercise B

1. table of contents   4. copyright page
2. index   5. glossary
3. appendix

Exercise C

(Answers may vary.)

1. microforms *or* vertical file
2. biographical reference
3. encyclopedia
4. atlas
5. almanac

Exercise D

(Answers may vary depending on the dictionaries used.)

1. roman—the upright style of printing; Roman—characteristic of ancient or modern Rome
2. hab-i-tat
3. verb, noun, adjective
4. architecture, sculpture, law, literature, drama, painting, geology, printing, baseball
5. It is a Hindi word meaning "dusty" or "dust colored."
6. anxiety
7. same
8. a sarcastic manner; all manner of things
9. third
10. cracker *or* cookie

Exercise E

1. R   2. I   3. T   4. I   5. T

Exercise F

5 1. Closing
6 2. Signature
4 3. Body
2 4. Inside address
1 5. Heading
3 6. Salutation

Exercise G

(Answers may vary.)

1. The letter should have been written sooner.
2. The letter is impolite.
3. The letter does not mention specifics about the product or problem.
4. The letter does not tell what the company can do to solve or correct the problem.

Exercise H

1. C   2. C   3. I   4. C   5. I

Exercise I

1. C   2. I   3. I   4. C   5. C

Exercise J: Proofreading

1. Egyptian writing dates to around 3300 B.C.

2. My aunt, M. E. Lightree, went to work for the Federal Bureau of Investigation in 1965, and now my cousin also works for the FBI.

3. Last week 2,579 people attended our first track meet.

4. When we flew to Dallas, Texas, the flight attendants were very nice to us.

5. When the helpers arrive, ask them to start sorting the books. [*or* When each helper arrives, ask him or her . . .]

Appendix: Diagraming Sentences

◆ WORKSHEET 1: DIAGRAMING SUBJECTS AND VERBS

Exercise

1. Angela | returned

2. She | was studying

3. (you) | Listen

4. She | enjoyed

5. you | Have been

◆ WORKSHEET 2: DIAGRAMING COMPOUND SUBJECTS AND COMPOUND VERBS

Exercise

1.

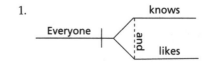

2.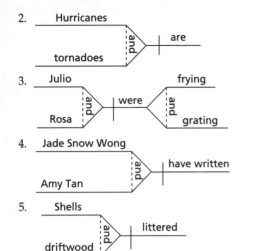

3.

4.

5.

◆ WORKSHEET 3: DIAGRAMING ADJECTIVES AND ADVERBS

Exercise

1.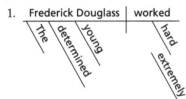

2.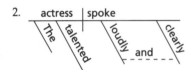

3.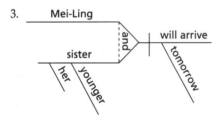

4.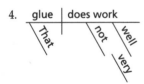

◆ WORKSHEET 4: DIAGRAMING DIRECT OBJECTS AND INDIRECT OBJECTS

Exercise

1.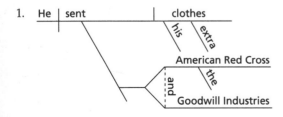

2.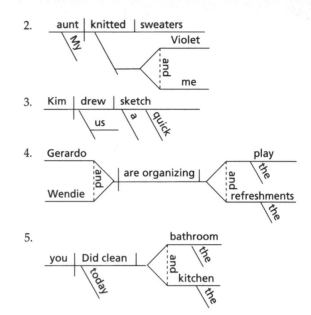

3.

4.

5.

◆ WORKSHEET 5: DIAGRAMING SUBJECT COMPLEMENTS

Exercise

1. Turtles | are \ reptiles

2.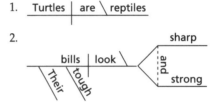

3. Turtles | may grow \ old — very

4. this | Is \ turtle — the largest freshwater

5. turtles | do look | painted — Painted really

◆ WORKSHEET 6: DIAGRAMING PREPOSITIONAL PHRASES

Exercise

1.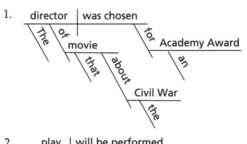

2.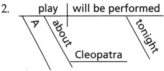

3.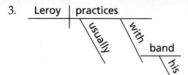
Leroy | practices / usually \ with \ band \ his

4.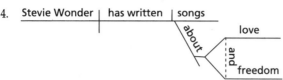
Stevie Wonder | has written | songs \ about < love / and \ freedom

5.
I | admire | paintings \ the \ of Marc Chagall

◆ WORKSHEET 7: DIAGRAMING SUBORDINATE CLAUSES

Exercise

1.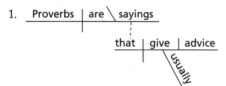
Proverbs | are \ sayings
that | give | advice \ usually

2.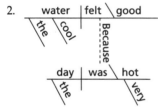
water | felt \ good \ the \ cool \ Because
day | was \ hot \ the \ very

3.
we | will visit | Crater Lake
it | does rain \ not \ if \ tomorrow

4.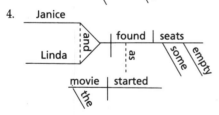
Janice
and
Linda | found | seats \ some \ empty \ as
movie | started \ the

5.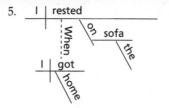
I | rested \ on \ sofa \ the \ When
I | got \ home

◆ WORKSHEET 8: DIAGRAMING SENTENCES CLASSIFIED BY STRUCTURE

Exercise

1.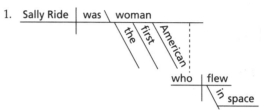
Sally Ride | was \ woman \ the \ first \ American
who | flew \ in space

2.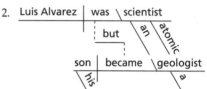
Luis Alvarez | was \ scientist \ an \ atomic
but
son | became \ geologist \ his \ a

3.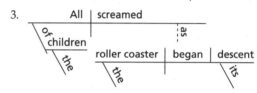
All | screamed \ of \ children \ the \ as
roller coaster | began | descent \ the \ its

4.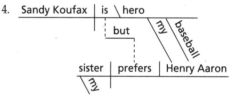
Sandy Koufax | is \ hero \ my \ baseball
but
sister | prefers | Henry Aaron \ my